Microsoft Excel Functions Quick Reference

For High-Quality Data Analysis, Dashboards, and More

Mandeep Mehta

Apress®

Microsoft Excel Functions Quick Reference: For High-Quality Data Analysis, Dashboards, and More

Mandeep Mehta
Mumbai, India

ISBN-13 (pbk): 978-1-4842-6612-0   ISBN-13 (electronic): 978-1-4842-6613-7
https://doi.org/10.1007/978-1-4842-6613-7

Managing Director, Apress Media LLC: Welmoed Spahr
Acquisitions Editor: Smriti Srivastava
Development Editor: Matthew Moodie
Coordinating Editor: Shrikant Vishwakarma

Cover designed by eStudioCalamar

Cover image designed by Pexels

Distributed to the book trade worldwide by Springer Science+Business Media LLC, 1 New York Plaza, Suite 4600, New York, NY 10004. Phone 1-800-SPRINGER, fax (201) 348-4505, email orders-ny@springer-sbm.com, or visit www.springeronline.com. Apress Media, LLC is a California LLC and the sole member (owner) is Springer Science+Business Media Finance Inc (SSBM Finance Inc). SSBM Finance Inc is a **Delaware** corporation.

For information on translations, please e-mail booktranslations@springernature.com; for reprint, paperback, or audio rights, please e-mail bookpermissions@springernature.com.

Apress titles may be purchased in bulk for academic, corporate, or promotional use. eBook versions and licenses are also available for most titles. For more information, reference our Print and eBook Bulk Sales web page at http://www.apress.com/bulk-sales.

Any source code or other supplementary material referenced by the author in this book is available to readers on GitHub via the book's product page, located at www.apress.com/978-1-4842-6612-0. For more detailed information, please visit http://www.apress.com/source-code.

Printed on acid-free paper

Dedicated to God and my family

Table of Contents

TABLE OF CONTENTS

About the Author

Mandeep Mehta has more than twenty years of experience in administration, operations, software development, and reporting. He mostly works with cross-functional teams in ensuring operational and service excellence. Mandeep has worked with Capgemini for ten years and is currently working as a freelancer, conducting various trainings in MS Office and providing data services.

About the Technical Reviewer

 **Mark Proctor** is a senior finance professional, qualified accountant, and blogger who has been applying spreadsheet-based solutions to real-world problems for the last twenty years. He has built a variety of Excel-based reporting, predictive, decision-making, and automation tools for achieving process efficiency in multinational companies in the media, food, retail, and manufacturing sectors. He is also the owner of *Excel Off the Grid* (`https://exceloffthegrid.com`), one of the most popular Excel blogs on the internet, which focuses on teaching intermediate and advanced Excel techniques.

Acknowledgments

I would like to begin by thanking God and my family. I would also like to the Apress team: Smriti Srivastava (acquisitions editor), Shrikant Vishwakarma (coordinating editor), Matthew Moodie (development editor), and everyone at Apress who has helped in this book.

I would also like to thank Mark Proctor, who has been helpful with his invaluable technical reviews and comments. Your feedback was very helpful.

My thanks also go out to my managers and colleagues at my workplaces, who encouraged me to share my Excel knowledge and enabled me to take trainings to share my Excel knowledge. This book is a result of your encouragement.

Last but not least, I would like to thank you, my readers.

Introduction

Having knowledge of Excel functions gives you an edge in your corporate life. The various Excel functions allow Excel users to create informational reports, useful dashboard models, and much more. Excel contains a lot of functions, and you could spend quite some time learning which functions work best for certain tasks and when to combine functions with other functions.

This is where this book comes in. This book will help you

- understand the different categories of Excel functions and how to use them; and
- how to combine functions to accomplish the tasks on hand.

As you gain proficiency in Excel functions, not only will you become more productive, but you will also be able to do tasks that you didn't know could be handled with Excel formulas.

Book Audience

This is not a book for beginners in Excel. It is for somebody who knows how to do the following:

- Create a workbook
- Add/delete worksheets
- Navigate within a workbook

- Use the ribbon and the dialog boxes that pop up in Excel

- Perform basic Windows activities like file management and copy-paste

This book will help you understand the various functions in Excel. For advanced users, this book can act as a reference book.

How Is the Book Organized?

The book is divided into chapters as follows:

- Chapter 1 introduces you to Excel functions.

- Chapter 2 shows you the TEXT functions in Excel.

- Chapters 3 and 4 show you the DATE and TIME functions in Excel.

- Chapter 5 introduces you named ranges and Excel tables.

- Chapter 6 focuses on LOOKUPS and REFERENCE functions in Excel.

- Chapter 7 brings in the AGGREGATE functions of Excel.

- Chapter 8 explores the LOGICAL functions in Excel.

- Chapter 9 visits some of the MATH functions in Excel.

- Chapter 10 explores the INFORMATION functions available in Excel.

- Chapter 11 gives an overview of the FINANCE functions of Excel.

- Chapter 12 talks about handling errors that arise while using Excel functions.

- Chapter 13 looks into megaformulas.

- Chapter 14 talks about ARRAY formulas in Excel.

I wish you good luck in using Excel functions, and I sincerely hope that you have as much fun with it as I did in writing this book.

CHAPTER 1

What Is an Excel Function?

A very warm welcome to all the readers of this book. You must be seeing many Excel files in your day-to-day lives. Every Excel file typically contains one or more of the following:

- Character data
- Numeric data
- Alphanumeric data
- Charts and images
- Excel functions

Since this book is about Excel functions, in this chapter we will look into what Excel functions are.

What Is an Excel Function?

An Excel function is a set piece of code built in Excel itself that performs certain predefined actions.

© Mandeep Mehta 2021
M. Mehta, *Microsoft Excel Functions Quick Reference,*
https://doi.org/10.1007/978-1-4842-6613-7_1

How to Use Excel Functions

All Excel formulas begin with an = or a + sign. An Excel formula can contain text and one or more Excel functions.

Every Excel function accepts zero or more arguments. Function arguments are given inside parentheses, separated by a comma. For example, an Excel function with arguments would look like

`FunctionName(argument1, argument2, ....).`

Here, `FunctionName` would be replaced by the actual name of the function. Arguments are the values that are passed to the functions. Multiple arguments are separated from one another by a comma (`,`). In some countries, the semicolon (`;`) is used to separate function arguments.

The arguments have to be of the correct data type for the function to work correctly. What this means is that if a function expects a date as an argument and you pass a text value, the function will give an error. The arguments can be

- a literal value of the correct data type,

- an Excel function returning the correct data type, or

- a cell reference where the cell contains the correct data type.

The cell reference can be one of the following:

- **Relative reference** - A relative reference is one where the row and column coordinates are not preceded by a $ sign, like A1 or A1:D100. By default, in Excel, cell references are relative. This is helpful when we move or copy formulas across multiple cells, as the relative references will change depending on the relative positions of the rows and columns. You will use relative references when you want to repeat the same calculation across multiple rows or columns.

- **Absolute reference** - An absolute reference is the one with the dollar sign ($) in the row coordinate, the column coordinate, or both the row and the column coordinates, like $A$1 or $A1 or A$1. An absolute cell reference remains unchanged when copying the formula to other cells. Absolute references are useful

  - when you want to perform calculations with a value in a specific cell, or

  - when you want to copy a formula to other cells without changing references.

Table 1-1 shows the different types of absolute references.

Table 1-1. *Absolute References*

Absolute Reference Type	Comment
$A1	Here, the column reference is fixed. The row reference is relative. So, when we copy a formula containing this type of reference, the column is always fixed but the row reference can change.
A$1	Here, the row reference is fixed. The column reference is relative. So, when we copy a formula containing this type of reference, the row is always fixed but the column reference can change.
$A$1	In this case, both the row and the column references are fixed. So, when we copy a formula containing this type of reference, both the row and the column are always fixed.

Types of Excel Functions

There are two types of Excel functions, as follows:

- **Volatile functions** – Some Excel functions are "volatile." Volatile functions are recalculated on every worksheet change. This can have a drastic impact on worksheet performance. In workbooks that contain a small amount of data, the performance impact may not be noticeable. But in workbooks that have a large amount of data and many formulas, a volatile function can slow down the worksheet.

- **Non-volatile functions** – Unlike volatile functions, non-volatile functions are not recalculated on every worksheet change. Non-volatile functions are recalculated when the data on which they depend changes. Some situations when this happens are as follows:

  - Entering new data

  - Modifying existing data

  - Deleting or inserting a row or a column

  - Renaming a worksheet

  - Hiding or unhiding rows (but not columns)

Categories of Excel Functions

Excel functions are grouped into various categories, like the following:

- Text functions

- Date functions

- Time functions

- Aggregate functions

- Logical functions

- Reference functions

- Math functions

- Information functions

Each of these categories will be covered in a chapter of its own. We will also briefly look into what mega-formulas and array formulas are.

Summary

In this chapter, we looked into the following:

- What an Excel function is

- How to use an Excel function

- Different categories of Excel functions

In the next chapter, we will look into text functions.

CHAPTER 2

Text Functions

In this chapter, we will look into the text functions provided by Excel.

Note In the text functions in this chapter, the argument text can be

- a literal text string value enclosed in double quotes (" "),
- an Excel function returning a text string,
- a cell reference where the cell contains a text string, or
- a named range containing a text string.

Let us begin exploring the text functions.

LEFT Function

This function returns characters from the left side of a text string.

© Mandeep Mehta 2021
M. Mehta, *Microsoft Excel Functions Quick Reference*,
https://doi.org/10.1007/978-1-4842-6613-7_2

Syntax

=LEFT(*text, CharCount*)

This function takes the following arguments:

- The first argument is the text string from which characters are to be extracted.

- The second argument tells the number of characters to be extracted from the left side.

Example

Figure 2-1 shows examples of the LEFT function.

	A	B
1		
2	Mandeep Mehta	Mandeep
3		Mandeep

Figure 2-1. *LEFT function*

In cell B2, we have used the function as =LEFT("Mandeep Mehta", 7). The function returns the value *Mandeep*.

Now let us understand this function. We are telling Excel to return seven characters from the left of the text *Mandeep Mehta*.

Similarly, in cell B3, we have used the function =LEFT(A2,7). This will also return the value *Mandeep*. The only difference between the formulas used in B2 and B3 is this: in the formula in B2 we have used a literal text value Mandeep Mehta, whereas, in the formula in B3 we have used the cell reference A2.

RIGHT Function

This function returns characters from the right side of a text string.

Syntax

=RIGHT(*text, CharCount*)

This function takes the following arguments:

- The first argument is the text from which characters are to be extracted.

- The second argument tells the number of characters to be extracted from the right side.

Example

Figure 2-2 shows examples of the RIGHT function.

◢	A	B
1		
2	Mandeep Mehta	Mehta
3		Mehta

Figure 2-2. *RIGHT function*

In cell B2, we have used the function as =RIGHT("Mandeep Mehta", 5). The function returns the value *Mehta*.

Now let us understand this function. We are telling Excel to return five characters from the right of the text *Mandeep Mehta*.

Similarly, in cell B3, we have used the function =RIGHT(A2,5). This will also return the value *Mehta*.

Here again, the only difference between the formulas used in B2 and B3 is this: in the formula in B2 we have used a literal text value, Mandeep Mehta, whereas in the formula in B3 we have used the cell reference A2.

MID Function

This function returns a set of characters from a text string, starting from a given position.

Syntax

=MID(*text, position, CharCount*)

This function takes the following arguments:

- The first argument is the text string from which characters are to be extracted.

- The second argument is the position from which the extraction is to start.

- The third argument is the number of characters to be extracted starting from the position mentioned in the second argument.

Example

Figure 2-3 shows an example of the MID function.

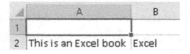

Figure 2-3. *MID function*

In cell B2, we have used the function =MID(A2, 12, 5). This will return the value *Excel*.

Here, we are telling the MID function to return five characters starting from the twelfth character of the text in cell A2.

UPPER Function

The UPPER function converts text from lowercase to uppercase.

Syntax

=UPPER(*text*)

The UPPER function expects only one argument:

- The text to be converted to uppercase

If the text is already in uppercase, no conversion happens.

Example

Figure 2-4 shows examples of the UPPER function.

◢	A	B
1		
2	mandeep mehta	MANDEEP MEHTA
3	MANDEEP MEHTA	MANDEEP MEHTA

Figure 2-4. *UPPER function*

The formula used in cell B2 is =UPPER(A2). This will return the value *MANDEEP MEHTA*. Since the text in A2 is in lowercase, the function in B2 returns the value in uppercase.

11

The formula used in cell B3 is =UPPER(A3). This will also return the value *MANDEEP MEHTA*. Since the text in A3 is already in uppercase, the function in B3 returns the value as it is, without any conversion.

LOWER Function

The LOWER function converts text from uppercase to lowercase.

Syntax

=LOWER(*text*)

The LOWER function expects only one argument:

- The text to be converted to lowercase

If the text is already in lowercase, no conversion happens.

Example

Figure 2-5 shows an example of the LOWER function.

	A	B
1		
2	MANDEEP MEHTA	mandeep mehta

Figure 2-5. *LOWER function*

The formula used in cell B2 is =LOWER(A2). This will return the value *mandeep mehta*. Since the text in A2 is in uppercase, the function in B2 returns the value in lowercase.

PROPER Function

The PROPER function converts the first character of all words in a sentence to uppercase and the remaining characters to lowercase.

Syntax

=PROPER(*text*)

The PROPER function expects only one argument:

- The text to be converted to proper case

If the text is already in proper case, no conversion happens.

Example

Figure 2-6 shows an example of the PROPER function.

▲	A	B
1		
2	This is text	This Is Text

Figure 2-6. *PROPER function*

The formula used in cell B2 is =PROPER(A2). This will return the value *This Is Text*.

TRIM Function

The TRIM function removes all extra whitespace from a text string, leaving only one space between words in the text. It removes Character 32 (standard space), but not Character 160 (which is an HTML break space). It also removes leading and trailing spaces.

13

Syntax

=TRIM(*text*)

The TRIM function expects only one argument, as follows:

- The text from which extra spaces are to be removed

Example

Figure 2-7 shows an example of the TRIM function.

	A	B
1		
2	This is Text containing spaces .	This is Text containing spaces .

Figure 2-7. *TRIM function*

The value in cell A2 is *This is Text containing spaces.* As you can see, it contains a lot of spaces. The formula in cell B2 is =TRIM(A2). This will return the value *This is Text containing spaces.* So, you can see the TRIM function has removed all the unwanted spaces from the text in cell A2.

LEN Function

The LEN function returns the length of a text.

Syntax

=LEN(*text*)

The LEN function expects only one argument, as follows:

- The text whose length is to be returned

14

Example

Figure 2-8 shows an example of the LEN function.

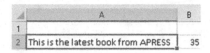

Figure 2-8. *LEN function*

The formula used in cell B2 is =LEN(A2). It returns the value *35*, which is the number of characters contained in the text in cell A2.

FIND Function

The FIND function is used to check if a text is found inside another text. It does a case-sensitive search. If the search is successful, it returns the position where the searched-for text begins. If the search fails, it returns *#VALUE!*

Syntax

=FIND(text to find, where to find, [starting from])

The FIND function takes the following arguments:

- The first argument is the text to be searched for.

- The second argument specifies in which text to search for the first argument.

- The third argument specifies from which position the search should start. This argument is optional. So, if it is not given, the search starts from the first position.

15

Example

Figure 2-9 shows an example of the FIND function.

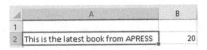

Figure 2-9. *FIND function*

The function used in cell B2 is =FIND("book", A2, 1). This will return the value *20*.

Let us see how this works. We are searching for the string *book* in the text in cell A2, which is *This is the latest book from APRESS*. Since the string *book* begins in the twentieth position in the text in cell A2, the FIND function returns the value *20*.

Now, try changing the function in cell B2 to =FIND("books", A2, 1). The FIND function will return the value *#VALUE!* since the string *books* does not occur in the text in cell A2.

Similarly, even if you change the function in cell B2 to =FIND("Book", A2, 1), the FIND function will return the value *#VALUE!* since the string *Book* does not occur in the text in cell A2. As you can see in this instance, case matters in the FIND function, as *book* is not the same as *Book*. The case of the letter *B* differs.

SEARCH Function

The SEARCH function is used to check if a text is found inside another text. The SEARCH function does a case-insensitive search. If the search is successful, it returns the position where the searched-for text begins. If the search fails, it returns *#VALUE!*

Syntax

=SEARCH(*text to find, where to find, [starting from]*)

The SEARCH function takes the following arguments:

- The first argument is the text to be searched for.

- The second argument specifies in which text to search for the first argument.

- The third argument specifies from which position the search should start. This argument is optional. So, if it is not given, the search starts from the first position.

Example

Figure 2-10 shows an example of the SEARCH function.

	A	B
1		
2	This is the latest book from APRESS	20

Figure 2-10. *SEARCH function*

The function used in cell B2 is =SEARCH ("book", A2, 1). This will return the value *20*.

Let us see how this works. We are searching for the string *book* in the text in cell A2, which is *This is the latest book from APRESS*. Since the string *book* begins in the twentieth position in the text in cell A2, the SEARCH function returns the value *20*.

Similarly, even if you change the function in cell B2 to =SEARCH ("Book", A2, 1), the SEARCH function will return the value *20*, since the string *Book* does occur in the text in cell A2. As you can see in this instance, case does not matter in the SEARCH function, as *book* is treated as the same as *Book*.

17

Now, try changing the function in cell B2 to =SEARCH ("books", A2, 1). The SEARCH function will return the value *#VALUE!* since the string *books* does not occur in the text in cell A2.

CONCATENATE/& Function

The CONCATENATE function is used to join two or more strings. The & operator is also used to join two or more strings. If you try to join a number using the CONCATENATE function, the number will be treated as text while performing the joining operations.

Syntax

=CONCATENATE(text1, text2, text3, ...)

The CONCATENATE function can take from 2 to 255 arguments. You would generally pass three to eight arguments in a normal scenario.

Example

Figure 2-11 shows an example of the CONCATENATE function.

◢	A	B	C
1			
2	My name is	Rahul	My name is Rahul

Figure 2-11. *CONCATENATE function*

In Figure 2-11, we have the text *My name is* in cell A2 and the text *Rahul* in cell B2. In cell C2, we have the function =CONCATENATE(A2," ",B2). This will return the value *My name is Rahul*.

We can also use the & operator in cell C2 instead of the CONCATENATE function, like =A2 & " " & B2. This will return the same result we got with the CONCATENATE function.

Note   If you join text and dates using the CONCATENATE function, the result might not be as expected, as can be seen in Figure 2-12.

◢	A	B	C
1			
2	Today is	22-08-2020	Today is 44065

Figure 2-12. *Mixing text and dates in CONCATENATE function*

The function used in cell C2 is =CONCATENATE(A2," ",B2). However the date in cell B2 is converted to a number in the result in cell C2. To get the date in the correct format, we need to use the TEXT function, which we will see shortly.

VALUE Function

The VALUE function converts a number in text format to an actual number. It gives a *#VALUE!* error if the argument is not a number represented in text format.

Some other ways to convert a number in text format to an actual number are by

- using the double negative sign; for example, =--"100"; or

- performing a simple arithmetic operation like adding a zero or multiplying by 1; for example:

  - ="100" + 0

  - ="100" * 1

19

Syntax

=VALUE(*text*)

The VALUE function expects only one argument, as follows:

- A text string representing number

Example

Figure 2-13 shows an example of the VALUE function.

	A	B
1		
2	100	100

Figure 2-13. *VALUE function*

The value in cell A2 is a text string representing the number 100. The function used in cell B2 is =VALUE(A2). The result will be the number *100*. As you can see, the value in cell B2 is right-aligned, just as a number should be in Excel.

TEXT Function

The TEXT function is used to convert a number or a date to text in a specified format. The TEXT function will return the error *#NAME?* if the quotation marks around the format code are missing.

Syntax

=TEXT(*value, format*)

The TEXT function expects the following arguments:

- The first argument is the number or date to be converted to a text string.

- The second argument is the format to which it is to be converted.

Note   There are different ways to write numbers in Excel, and their formats will vary depending on your region. For example, in the United States, decimal numbers are written with a period, like 5.65. However, in many countries, decimal numbers are written with a comma; for example, 5,65.

Similarly, there are variations with the thousands separator. In the United States, this is typically written with a comma; for example, 1,000. In other countries, it's often written like this: 1.000.

Table 2-1 shows the commonly used format codes for numbers.

Table 2-1. *Format Codes for Numbers*

Format Code	Comment	Example
0	Displays leading or trailing zeros that are omitted by Excel	000000.00 The value 12345.6789 will be displayed as 012345.68
#	Will ignore extra zeros	"###,####.##" The value 123456.6789 will be displayed as 123,456.68
Comma ','	Used for thousands separator	As used in the previous example
Dot '.'	Used for decimal separator	As used in the previous example

Note   In regions where the comma (',') is used as a decimal separator and the dot ('.') is used as a thousands separator, you could use a format like "###.###,##".

Table 2-2 shows format codes for date and time.

Table 2-2. *Format Codes for Date and Time*

Code	Comment
dd	Two-digit day of the month with leading zeros
d	Two-digit day of the month without leading zeros
ddd	Weekday name short form, Mon to Sun
dddd	Weekday name full form, Monday to Sunday
mm	Two-digit month with leading zeros
m	Two-digit month without leading zeros
mmm	Month name short form, Jan to Dec
mmmm	Month name full form, January to December
yy	Two-digit year
yyyy	Four-digit year
hh	Two-digit hour of the day with leading zeros
h	Two-digit hour of the day without leading zeros
mm	Two-digit minute with leading zeros, when used in time
m	Two-digit minute without leading zeros, when used in time
ss	Two-digit seconds with leading zeros
s	Two-digit seconds without leading zeros

Example

Figure 2-14 gives examples of TEXT functions.

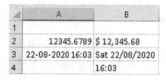

Figure 2-14. *TEXT functions*

Table 2-3 gives the values and functions used in the cells shown in Figure 2-14.

Table 2-3. *Values and Functions Used in Figure 2-14*

Cell A2 value	12345.6789	Cell B2 function	=TEXT(A2, "$ ###,###.##")
Cell A3 value	22-08-2020 16:03:36	Cell B3 function	=TEXT(A3, "ddd dd/mm/yyyy")
		Cell B4 function	=TEXT(A3, "hh:mm")

EXACT Function

The EXACT function is used to check if two text strings are an exact match. If the text strings match, it returns *TRUE*; else it returns *FALSE*.

Syntax

```
=EXACT(text1, text2)
```

The EXACT function expects two arguments: the two text strings that are to be compared.

23

Example

Figure 2-15 shows an example of the EXACT function.

	A	B	C
1			
2	Mandeep	Mandeep	TRUE
3	Mandeep	mandeep	FALSE

Figure 2-15. *EXACT function*

The values in cells A2 and A3 are both *Mandeep*. The value in cell B2 is *Mandeep*, and the value in cell B3 is *mandeep*. The function used in cell C2 is =EXACT(A2,B2). It returns the value *TRUE*, as the values in cells A2 and B2 are the same. The function used in cell C3 is =EXACT(A3,B3). It returns the value *FALSE* because the values in cells A3 and B3 are different, as a result of the case of the letter *m* in cells A3 and B3.

REPLACE Function

The REPLACE function is used to replace part of a text string with another string.

Syntax

=REPLACE(*Text1, start position, number of characters to replace, replacement text*)

The REPLACE function expects four arguments, as follows:

- The first argument is the text string where replacement will happen.

- The second argument is the position from where the replacement will start.

- The third argument is the number of characters to be replaced.

- The fourth argument is the replacement text to be used for replacement.

Example

Figure 2-16 shows an example of the REPLACE function.

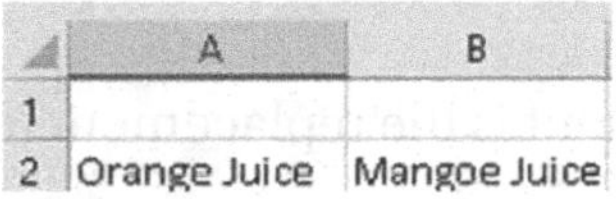

Figure 2-16. *REPLACE function*

Cell A2 contains the value *Orange Juice*. In cell B2, the function used is =REPLACE(A2, 1, 5, "Mango"). This will return the value *Mangoe Juice*. Let us understand the function in cell B2. We are telling Excel to replace the text in cell A2, starting from first position and replacing five characters, with the value *Mango*. So basically, what is happening is that the text *Orang* is replaced with *Mango*. If you wanted to replace the entire word *Orange* with *Mango*, the function in cell B2 would look like this: =REPLACE(A2, 1, 6, "Mango").

SUBSTITUTE Function

The SUBSTITUTE function is used to replace a string with another string. The search is case sensitive for this function.

Syntax

```
=SUBSTITUTE(Text1, search text, new text, [which instance to be
replaced])
```

The SUBSTITUTE function takes the following arguments:

- The first argument is the text string where the search will happen.

- The second argument is the text string to be searched for.

- The third argument is the replacement text.

- The fourth argument tells which occurrence of the text string mentioned in the second argument is to be replaced. This argument is optional. If this argument is not given, all occurrences of the text string mentioned in the second argument are replaced.

Examples

Figure 2-17 shows an example of the SUBSTITUTE function.

⊿	A	B
1		
2	Round and Round	circle and circle
3	Round and Round	Round and circle

Figure 2-17. SUBSTITUTE function

The function used in cell B2 is =SUBSTITUTE(A2,"Round","circle"). The value returned is *circle and circle*. Here, we are telling Excel to replace all instances of *Round* with *circle*. Since the fourth argument is missing, all instances are replaced.

In Figure 2-17, the function used in cell B3 is =SUBSTITUTE(A2,"Round", "circle", 2). The value returned is *Round and circle*. Here, we are telling Excel to replace the second instance of *Round* with *circle*, since the fourth argument has the value *2*, indicating the second instance.

REPT Function

The REPT function repeats a text the given number of times.

Syntax

=REPT(text, number of times)

The REPT function expects two arguments, as follows:

- The first argument is the text to repeat.

- The second argument is the number of times the text is to be repeated.

Example

Figure 2-18 shows an example of the REPT function.

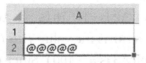

Figure 2-18. *REPT function*

The function used in cell A2 is =REPT("@", 5). The value returned is @@@@@. So, we are telling Excel to repeat the @ character five times.

27

T Function

The T function checks if the argument passed to it is text. If the argument is text, it returns the text as it is. If the argument is not text, it returns an empty string.

Syntax

=T(*text*)

The T function expects only one argument, as follows:

- The value to be checked as to whether it is text or not

Example

Figure 2-19 gives examples of the T function.

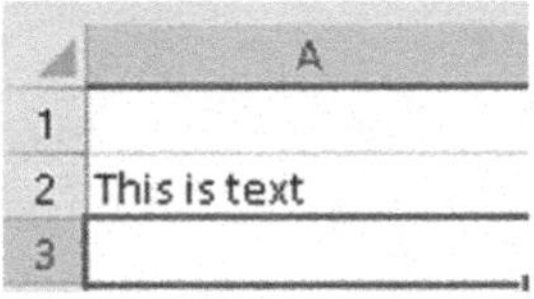

Figure 2-19. *T function*

The function used in cell A2 is =T("This is text"). Since the argument is a text string, it returns the value *This is text*.

The function used in cell A3 is =T(100). Since the argument is not a text string, it returns a blank value.

TEXTJOIN Function

The TEXTJOIN function joins text from multiple ranges and/or literal strings. The text is separated by a specified delimiter.

Note   The TEXTJOIN function is available only in Microsoft 365 and Office 2019.

Syntax

=TEXTJOIN(*delimiter, ignore_empty, text1*, [*text2, ... text_n*])

The TEXTJOIN function takes the following arguments:

- The first argument is the delimiter used to separate the joined text.

- The second argument determines if empty values are to be included in the resulting string. This argument can take the following values:

  - *TRUE* - ignores empty values in the result

  - *FALSE* - includes empty values in the result

- Text1 to text_n are the strings that you wish to join together. You can have up to 252 strings that can be joined together.

Example

Figure 2-20 shows examples of the TEXTJOIN function.

	A	B	C	D
1	First Name	Middle Name	Last Name	Full Name
2	Sachin	Ramesh	Tendulkar	Sachin Ramesh Tendulkar
3	Chris	H	Gayle	Chris H Gayle
4	Amitabh		Bachchan	Amitabh Bachchan
5	Shahrukh		Khan	Shahrukh Khan

Figure 2-20. *TEXTJOIN function*

In cell D2, we have used the function =TEXTJOIN(" ", TRUE,A2:C2). This will join first name, middle name, and last name to form the full name. The full name text is separated by a space. Copy the formula in cell D2 to the cells D3 to D5. As you can see in Figure 2-20, the middle name is blank in cells B4 and B5. And in the formula in cells D2 to D5 we have used TRUE as the second parameter, indicating that blank values are to be ignored. Hence, the values in cells D4 and D5 only have the first name and the last name.

Summary

To summarize, in this chapter we looked at some of the TEXT functions provided by Excel. I suggest you try out the examples from this chapter using your own data. This will give you more clarity regarding how the functions actually work.

In the next chapter, we will look at date functions.

CHAPTER 3

Date Functions

In this chapter, we will look at date functions provided by Excel.

Note In the date functions in this chapter, the argument date can be

- a literal date value,

- an Excel function returning a date,

- a cell reference where the cell contains a date, or

- a named range containing a date.

Excel internally considers dates as sequential numbers so that calculations can be done easily. It is the formatting of the cells that causes a number to be displayed as a date or time or date and time. Most of the date functions used in this chapter return a serial number. So, you are advised to format the cells to a proper date format wherever these data functions are used, so that dates appear as dates and not as numbers.

Let us begin exploring the most commonly used date functions.

© Mandeep Mehta 2021
M. Mehta, *Microsoft Excel Functions Quick Reference*,
https://doi.org/10.1007/978-1-4842-6613-7_3

TODAY Function

The TODAY function returns the current system date.

Syntax

`=TODAY()`

This function does not take any argument.

Example

Figure 3-1 shows an example of the TODAY function.

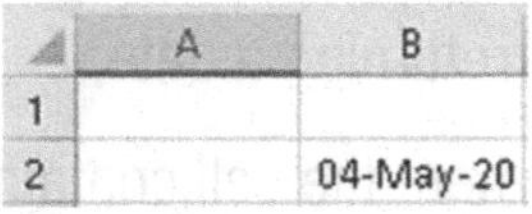

◢	A	B
1		
2		04-May-20

Figure 3-1. *TODAY function*

In cell B2, we have used the TODAY function. This function returns the value *04-May-20*, assuming the system date is May 4, 2020. You can format cell B2 to your liking as far as the display of the date format is concerned.

DAY Function

The DAY function returns the day component of a date.

Syntax

`=DAY(date)`

The DAY function expects only one argument, as follows:

- The date from which the day component is to be extracted

The return value can be a value between 1 and 31, depending on the month.

The *date* argument should be a valid date. If the *date* argument is not a date, the DAY function returns the error *#VALUE!*.

Example

Figure 3-2 gives an example of the DAY function.

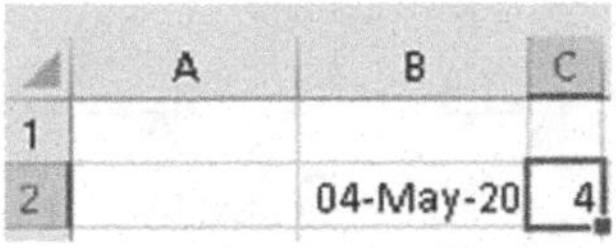

Figure 3-2. *DAY function*

The function in cell C2 is =DAY(B2). The value returned is *4.* Here, we are telling Excel to return the day component of the date contained in cell B2. As you can see in Figure 3-2, cell B2 contains the value *04-May-20.* Since the DAY function returns the day component of a date, the function in cell C2 returns the value *4.*

MONTH Function

The MONTH function returns the month component of a date.

Syntax

=MONTH(*date*)

The MONTH function expects only one argument, as follows:

- The date from which the month component is to be extracted

The return value can be a value between 1 and 12, depending on the month.

The *date* argument should be a valid date. If the *date* argument is not a date, the MONTH function returns the error *#VALUE!*.

Example

Figure 3-3 shows an example of the MONTH function.

◢	A	B	C
1			
2		04-May-20	5

Figure 3-3. *MONTH function*

The function in cell C2 is =MONTH(B2). The value returned is 5. Here, we are telling Excel to return the month component of the date contained in cell B2. As you can see in Figure 3-3, cell B2 contains the value *04-May-20*. Since the MONTH function returns the month component of a date, the function in cell C2 returns the value *5*.

YEAR Function

The YEAR function returns the year component of a date.

Syntax

=YEAR(*date*)

The YEAR function expects only one argument, as follows:

- The date from which the year component is to be extracted

The return value will be the year component of the date passed.

The *date* argument should be a valid date. If the *date* argument is not a date, the YEAR function returns the error *#VALUE!*.

Example

Figure 3-4 shows an example of the YEAR function.

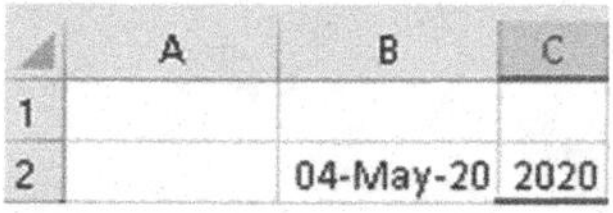

Figure 3-4. *YEAR function*

The function in cell C2 is =YEAR(B2). The value returned is *2020*. Here, we are telling Excel to return the year component of the date contained in cell B2. As you can see in Figure 3-4, cell B2 contains the value *04-May-20*. Since the YEAR function returns the year component of a date, the function in cell C2 returns the value *2020*.

EDATE Function

The EDATE function returns a date that is a specified number of months in the past or in the future.

Syntax

=EDATE(*date, number of months*)

The EDATE function expects two arguments:

- The first argument is a date.

- The second argument is number of months to add or subtract to the date given in the first argument. If a positive number is used for the second argument, you get a date after the date argument. If a negative number is used for the second argument, you get a date that will be before the date argument.

The EDATE function will give an error if any of the arguments are not of the expected data type.

Example

Figure 3-5 shows an example of the EDATE function.

▲	A	B	C
1			
2		04-May-20	04-Oct-20
3			04-Dec-19

Figure 3-5. EDATE function

Cell B2 contains the value *04-May-20*.

The function used in cell C2 is =EDATE(B2,5). Here, we are telling Excel to return a date five months after 04-May-20. So, the value returned is *04-Oct-20*. Remember to correctly format cell C2 to your preferred date format, or the function will return a numeric value *44108*, which is how "04-Oct-20" is internally represented in Excel.

The function used in cell C3 is =EDATE(B2,-5). Here, we are telling Excel to return a date five months before 04-May-20. So, the value returned is *04-Dec-19*. Remember to correctly format cell C3 to your preferred date format, or the function will return a numeric value *43803*, which is how "04-Dec-19" is internally represented in Excel.

EOMONTH Function

The EOMONTH function returns the last day of the month that is a given number of months before or after a given date.

Syntax

=EOMONTH(*date, number of months*)

The EOMONTH function expects two arguments:

- The first argument is a date.

- The second argument is months to add or subtract to the date given in the first argument. If a positive number is used for the second argument, you get a date that will be after the date argument. If a negative number is used for the second argument, you get a date that will be before the date argument.

Example

Figure 3-6 shows examples of the EOMONTH function.

◢	A	B	C
1			
2		04-May-20	31-Oct-20
3			31-Dec-19
4			31-May-20

Figure 3-6. *EOMONTH function*

Cell B2 contains the value *04-May-20*.

In cell C2, the function used is =EOMONTH(B2,5). The value returned is *31-Oct-20*. Let us understand how this works. The EOMONTH function works in two steps, as follows:

- First, we tell Excel to give a date five months from the value in cell B2, which is *04-May-20*. So, we get the value *04-Oct-20*.

- Next is to get the last day of the month we got in step 1, which was October in step 1. So, the value we get in step 2 is *31-Oct-20*, which is the last day of October.

In cell C3, the function used is =EOMONTH(B2,-5). The value returned is *31-Dec-19*. Let us understand how this works. The EOMONTH function works in two steps, as follows:

- First, we tell Excel to give a date five months before the value in cell B2, which is *04-May-20*. So, we get the value *04-Dec-19*.

- Next is to get the last day of the month we got in step 1, which was December. So, the value we get in step 2 is *31-Dec-19*, which is the last day of December.

In cell C4, the function used is =EOMONTH(B2,0). The value returned is *31-May-20*. Let us understand how this works. The EOMONTH function works in two steps, as follows:

- First, we tell Excel to give a date zero months from the value in cell B2, which is *04-May-20*. Since we are using *0* for the second argument, we get the value *04-May-20*.

- When *0* is used for the second argument of the EOMONTH function, we are telling Excel to return the same date used in the first argument, which is *04-May-20* in this case.

- Next is to get the last day of the month we got in step 1, which was May. So, the value we get in step 2 is *31-May-20*, which is the last day of May.

WEEKDAY Function

The WEEKDAY function is used to return a day's position within the week from a date in a numeric format. The return value is a number from 1 to 7 or from 0 to 6.

Syntax

=WEEKDAY(*date*, [*return type*])

The WEEKDAY function takes the following arguments:

- The first argument is the date whose weekday is to be found out.

- The second argument, which is numeric, tells which day of the week to be considered the first day. This argument is optional. If this argument is omitted, the default return type of 1 is used.

Table 3-1 shows the most commonly used return-type values and the corresponding numbers returned.

Table 3-1. *Return Type and Corresponding Values*

Return Type	Corresponding Values
1 or omitted	Starts with 1 for Sunday and goes till 7 for Saturday
2	Starts with 1 for Monday till 7 for Sunday
3	Starts with 0 for Monday till 6 for Sunday
11	Starts with 1 for Monday till 7 for Sunday
12	Starts with 1 for Tuesday till 7 for Monday
13	Starts with 1 for Wednesday till 7 for Tuesday
14	Starts with 1 for Thursday till 7 for Wednesday
15	Starts with 1 for Friday till 7 for Thursday
16	Starts with 1 for Saturday till 7 for Friday
17	Starts with 1 for Sunday till 7 for Saturday

Note   Return types 1 and 2 are the most commonly used.

Example

Figure 3-7 shows examples of the WEEKDAY function.

▲	A	B	C
1			
2		04-May-20	2
3			1

Figure 3-7. *WEEKDAY function*

Cell B2 contains the value *04-May-20*.

In cell C2, we have used the function =WEEKDAY(B2). The value returned is 2. Let us examine this. As you might have noticed, we have skipped the second argument. So, the return type that will be used is 1 (refer to Table 3-1). The date 4-May-20 falls on a Monday, and since we have used the default return type of 1 (where Sunday is 1, Monday is 2, and so on), the value returned by the function in C2 is 2.

In cell C3, we have used the function =WEEKDAY(B2,2). The value returned is 1. Let us examine this. As you might have noticed, we have not skipped the second argument. So, the return type that will be used is 2 (refer to Table 3-1). The date 4-May-20 falls on a Monday, and since we have used the return type of 2 (where Monday is 1), the value returned by the function in C3 is 1.

Note   The return type can be confusing. Return type 2 is the more commonly used value, since it is easy to understand, in that a week starts on Monday.

WEEKNUM Function

The WEEKNUM function is used to return the week number of a given date.

Syntax

=WEEKNUM(*date*, [*return type*])

The WEEKNUM function takes the following arguments:

- The first argument is the date whose week number is required.

- The second argument is the return type, which tells which day the week begins with. This argument is optional. If this argument is omitted, then the return type 1 is used.

41

Table 3-2 gives the return types for the WEEKNUM function.

Table 3-2. *Return Types for WEEKNUM Function*

Return Type	Comment
1	Week starts on a Sunday; week that contains January 1 is the first week of the year.
2	Week starts on a Monday; week that contains January 1 is the first week of the year.
11	Week starts on a Monday; week that contains January 1 is the first week of the year.
12	Week starts on a Tuesday; week that contains January 1 is the first week of the year.
13	Week starts on a Wednesday; week that contains January 1 is the first week of the year.
14	Week starts on a Thursday; week that contains January 1 is the first week of the year.
15	Week starts on a Friday; week that contains January 1 is the first week of the year.
16	Week starts on a Saturday; week that contains January 1 is the first week of the year.
17	Week starts on a Sunday; week that contains January 1 is the first week of the year.
21	Week starts on a Monday; week that contains first Thursday of the year is the first week of the year. This is also known as the European week-numbering system.

Example

Figure 3-8 shows an example of the WEEKNUM function.

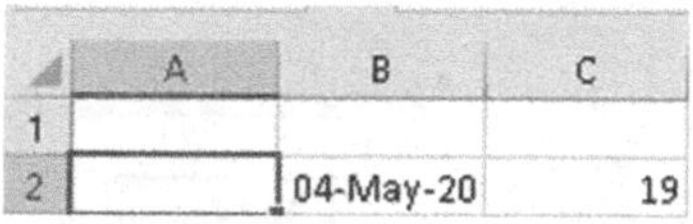

Figure 3-8. *WEEKNUM function*

Cell B2 contains the value *04-May-20*. In cell C2, we have used the function =WEEKNUM(B2,2). The value returned is *19*. Here, *19* indicates the nineteenth week of the year 2020.

DATE Function

The DATE function is used to create a date using the year, month, and day specified by the user.

Syntax

=DATE(*year, month, day*)

The DATE function expects three arguments, as follows:

- The first argument is the year in numeric format.

- The second argument is the month in numeric format.

- The third argument is the day in numeric format.

Using the year, month, and day that you give, the DATE function will create a date.

Example

Figure 3-9 shows an example of the DATE function.

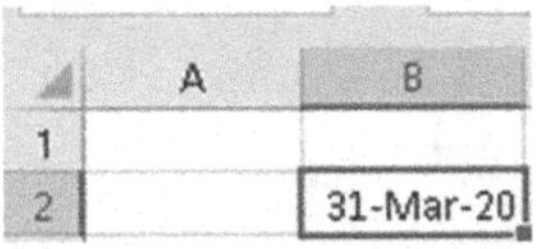

Figure 3-9. *DATE function*

In cell B2, we have used the function =DATE(2020,3,31). This will return the date March 31, 2020. Cell B2 is formatted with the format "dd-mmm-yy"; hence, you see "31-Mar-20" in cell B2 in Figure 3-9.

DATEVALUE Function

The DATEVALUE function is used to create a date from a text string that is in a correct date format.

Syntax

=DATEVALUE(*text*)

The DATEVALUE function expects only one argument, as follows:

- A text string in an acceptable date format

Example

Figure 3-10 shows an example of the DATEVALUE function:

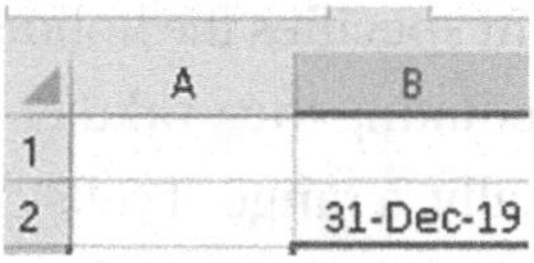

Figure 3-10. *DATEVALUE function*

In cell B2, we have used the function =DATEVALUE("31-Dec-2019").
This will return a correctly formatted date value, as can be seen in cell B2.

WORKDAY Function

The WORKDAY function is used to calculate a date that is a specified
number of workdays in the past or in the future based on a given date. It
will exclude the following:

- weekends, excluded by default

- holidays that you specify in the third argument

The WORKDAY function is useful for calculating due dates based on a
five-day work week from Monday to Friday.

Syntax

=WORKDAY(*date, number of workdays, [holiday list]*)

The WORKDAY function takes the following arguments

- The first argument is the start date for the workday
  calculation.

- The second argument is the number of workdays to
  add or subtract from the start date given in the first
  argument. A positive number returns a date after the
  date argument, and a negative number returns a date
  before the *date* argument.

- The third argument specifies the holidays to be ignored while calculating the workday. This argument is optional. Generally, a range of cells containing the dates to be ignored is used for the third argument.

Example

Figure 3-11 shows examples of the WORKDAY function.

◢	A	B	C	D	E
1					
2		24-Apr-20	26-May-20		01-May-20
3					13-May-20

Figure 3-11. *WORKDAY function*

In cell C2, we have used the function =WORKDAY(B2, 20, E2:E3). This gives us the value *26-May-20*. Let us understand how all this works.

- The first argument to the WORKDAY function is the start date, *24-Apr-20*, which comes from cell B2.

- The second argument is *20*. This means we want the twentieth workday, starting from 24-Apr-20.

- The third argument is the holiday dates to be ignored. These are given by the range E2:E3 in the function. For this example, we have assumed that May 1 and May 13, 2020, are holidays. To keep the example simple, I have used only two holidays. Your holiday list could be a bigger range.

So, we are telling Excel to count twenty working days starting from April 24, 2020, ignoring the holidays on May 1 and 13, 2020. This gives us the value of *26-May-20*.

NETWORKDAYS Function

The NETWORKDAYS function gives the number of workdays between two dates while at the same time ignoring holidays that are given to the function. Weekends are excluded by default.

Syntax

=NETWORKDAYS(*start date, end date, [holiday list]*)

The NETWORKDAYS function takes the following arguments:

- The first argument is the start date from which to start counting the workdays.

- The second argument is the end date up to which counting of workdays is to be done.

- The third argument, which is optional, is the list of dates to be ignored for the calculation.

Both the start date and end date are counted when calculating the number of days.

Example

Figure 3-12 shows an example of the NETWORKDAYS function.

⊿	A	B	C	D	E
1					Holiday list
2	Start Date	24-Apr-20	21		01-May-20
3	End Date	26-May-20			13-May-20

Figure 3-12. *NETWORKDAYS function*

Cell B2 contains the start date, and cell B3 contains the end date. Cells E2 and E3 contain the holiday dates. In cell C2, we have used the function =NETWORKDAYS(B2,B3,E2:E3). This returns the value *21*. Here, we are telling Excel to count the number of workdays between 24-Apr-20 and 26-May-20, excluding weekends and the dates specified in cells E2 and E3. To keep the example simple, I have used only two holidays. Your holiday list could be a bigger range.

DATEDIF Function

The DATEDIF function is used to calculate the difference between two dates in terms of days, months, and years.

Note   Excel's functions window does not recognize this as a valid formula. This function was added for compatibility with Lotus 1-2-3 back when Excel was first launched.

Syntax

=DATEDIF(start date, end date, unit of conversion)

The DATEDIF function expects three arguments, as follows:

- The first argument is the start date.

- The second argument is the end date.

- The third argument specifies how the conversion has to be done: in days, months, or years.

Table 3-3 shows the conversion units that can be used as the third argument and their meanings.

Table 3-3. *Conversion Units*

Conversion Unit	Returns
d	Number of days between the start date and the end date
m	Number of completed months between the start date and the end date
y	Number of completed years between the start date and the end date
md	Number of days between the start date and the end date, ignoring the months
ym	Number of months between the start date and the end date, ignoring the days and the years
yd	Number of days between the start date and the end date, ignoring the months and the years

Example

Figure 3-13 shows examples of DATEDIF functions.

⬚	A	B	C
1			
2	14-Jun-16	19-Dec-19	1283
3			42
4			3
5			5
6			6
7			188

Figure 3-13. *DATEDIF function*

In Figure 3-13, cell A2 contains the start date of "14-Jun-16" and cell B2 contains the end date of "19-Dec-19." Table 3-4 shows the formula used in cells from C2 to C7.

Table 3-4. *Formula Used in Cells C2 to C7 in Figure 3-13*

Cell	Formula Used	Value	Explanation
C2	=DATEDIF(A2,B2,"d")	1283	*1283* is the difference in days between the start and end dates.
C3	=DATEDIF(A2,B2,"m")	42	*42* is the difference in months between the start and end dates.
C4	=DATEDIF(A2,B2,"y")	3	*3* is the difference in years between the start and end dates.
C5	=DATEDIF(A2,B2,"md")	5	*5* is the difference in days between the start and end dates, ignoring the months and years. This is calculated as 19th day minus 14th day.
C6	=DATEDIF(A2,B2,"ym")	6	*6* is the difference in months between the start and end dates, ignoring the days and years. 6 is the difference between the months June (6th month) and December (12th month).
C7	=DATEDIF(A2,B2,"yd")	188	*188* is the difference in days between the start and end dates, ignoring the years in between. 188 is the difference in days between 14-Jun and 19-Dec.

Summary

To summarize, in this chapter we looked at some of the date functions provided by Excel. As always, I suggest you try out the examples from this chapter using your own data and also using the different options for the arguments. This will give you more clarity regarding how the functions actually work.

In the next chapter, we will look at time functions provided by Excel.

CHAPTER 4

Time Functions

In this chapter, we will look at some of the commonly used time functions provided by Excel.

Note   In the time functions in this chapter, the argument *time* can be

- a literal date-time value,
- an Excel function returning a date-time,
- a cell reference where the cell contains a date-time, or
- a named range containing a date-time value.

Let us begin exploring the most commonly used time functions.

NOW Function

The NOW function returns the system date and time at the point this function is executed.

Syntax

```
=NOW()
```

The NOW function does not take any argument.

© Mandeep Mehta 2021
M. Mehta, *Microsoft Excel Functions Quick Reference*,
https://doi.org/10.1007/978-1-4842-6613-7_4

Example

Figure 4-1 shows an example of the NOW function.

⩔	A	B
1		
2		24-08-2020 16:26

Figure 4-1. *NOW function*

In cell B2 we have used the function =NOW(). If you try out this function on your system, it will give a different output.

HOUR Function

The HOUR function returns the hour part from a date-time value. The value returned will be between 0 and 23. The hour is always returned in 24-hour format.

Syntax

=HOUR(*date-time*)

The HOUR function expects only one argument, as follows:

- A date-time value containing a time component

Example

Figure 4-2 shows an example of the HOUR function.

⩔	A	B	C
1			
2		24-08-2020 16:43:15	
3			16

Figure 4-2. *HOUR function*

Cell B2 contains the value *24-08-2020 16:43:15*. In cell C3, we have used the function =HOUR(B2). This will return the value *16*, the hour component.

MINUTE Function

The MINUTE function returns the minute part from a date-time value. The value returned will be between 0 and 59.

Syntax

=MINUTE(*date-time*)

The MINUTE function expects only one argument, as follows:

- A date-time value containing a time component

Example

Figure 4-3 shows an example of the MINUTE function.

⊿	A	B	C
1			
2		24-08-2020 16:43:15	
3			43

Figure 4-3. *MINUTE function*

Cell B2 contains the value *24-08-2020 16:43:15*. In cell C3, we have used the function =MINUTE(B2). This will return the value *43*, the minute component.

SECOND Function

The SECOND function returns the second part from a date-time value. The value returned will be between 0 and 59.

Syntax

`=SECOND(date-time)`

The SECOND function expects only one argument, as follows:

- A date-time value containing a time component

Example

Figure 4-4 shows an example of the SECOND function.

▲	A	B	C
1			
2		24-08-2020 16:43:15	
3			15

Figure 4-4. *SECOND function*

Cell B2 contains the value *24-08-2020 16:43:15*. In cell C3, we have used the function =SECOND(B2). This will return the value *15*, the seconds component.

TIME Function

The TIME function is used to create a time using the hour, minute, and second specified by the user.

Syntax

=TIME(*hour, minute, second*)

The TIME function expects three arguments, as follows:

- The first argument is the hour part in numeric format.

- The second argument is the minute part in numeric format.

- The third argument is the seconds part in numeric format.

Example

Figure 4-5 shows an example of the TIME function.

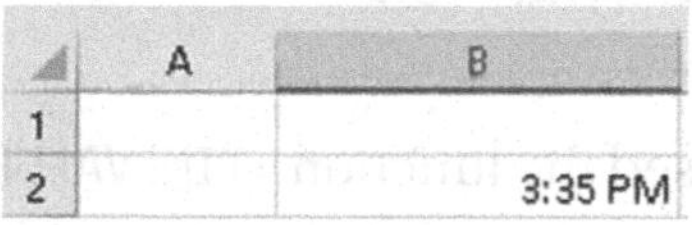

Figure 4-5. *TIME function*

In cell B2, we have used the function =TIME(15,35,20). This gives the value *3:35 PM*. Mind you, I have formatted cell B2 to make time appear in a human-understandable format. The format used for this example is "hh:mm AM/PM."

TIMEVALUE Function

The TIMEVALUE function is used to create a time using a text string in the correct format.

Syntax

=TIMEVALUE(*text*)

The TIMEVALUE function expects only one argument, as follows:

- A text string in an acceptable format for converting to time format

Example

Figure 4-6 shows an example of the TIMEVALUE function.

◢	A	B
1		
2		3:45:30 PM

Figure 4-6. *TIMEVALUE function*

In cell B2, we have used the function =TIMEVALUE("15:45:30"). This will create the value as shown in cell B2 in Figure 4-6. In this example, I have formatted cell B2 to show the value appropriately. The format used in cell B2, for this example, is "dd:mm:ss AM/PM."

Summary

To summarize, in this chapter we looked at some of the time functions provided by Excel. As always, I suggest you try out the examples from this chapter using your own data and also using the different options for the arguments. This will give you more clarity regarding how the functions actually work.

In the next chapter, we will look at Excel tables.

CHAPTER 5

Named Ranges and Excel Tables

In this chapter, we will look into what named ranges are, how to create one, and what their benefits are. Then, we will look into a powerful but often overlooked feature of Excel, the Excel table.

Named Ranges

A named range is when a name is given to a single cell, or to a range of cells. This name can be used

- instead of regular cell references in formulas,
- to define the source for graphs, and
- to define the data validation source.

Advantages of Named Ranges

Some of the advantages of named ranges are as follows:

- Formulas become easier to understand and debug.
- The creation of complicated spreadsheets becomes easy.
- They help to simplify your macros.

© Mandeep Mehta 2021
M. Mehta, *Microsoft Excel Functions Quick Reference*,
https://doi.org/10.1007/978-1-4842-6613-7_5

Create a Named Range

Figure 5-1 shows how to create a named range.

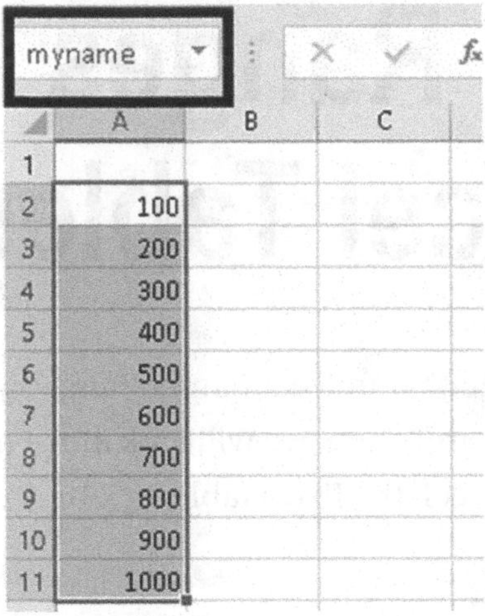

Figure 5-1. *Create a named range*

Here are the steps to create a named range:

1. Select the cell(s) that you want to name. In Figure 5-1, we have selected the range from A2 to A11.

2. Next, type a name in the *name* box, highlighted by a black border in Figure 5-1, and press the Enter key.

Another way to create a named range is by using the Name Manager. Figure 5-2 shows the Name Manager.

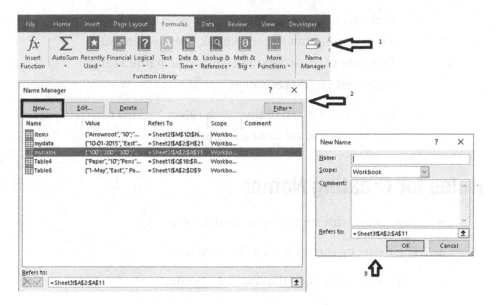

Figure 5-2. *Name Manager*

To get to the Name Manager, do the following:

1. Click on the Formulas tab in the ribbon, as shown
    by arrow 1.

2. Click on Name Manager. You get the Name Manager,
    as shown in Figure 5-2 at arrow 2.

3. To create a new named range, click on New in the
    Name Manager window. You get the New Name
    window, as shown by arrow 3 in Figure 5-2. Here
    you can supply the following:

    •   The name for the range

    •   The scope of the named range. The default
        is workbook, which means the name can be
        referenced anywhere in the current workbook.
        The other scope is the sheet name, which means
        the name can be referenced only in the selected

worksheet. To use a named range with a worksheet scope throughout the workbook, you need to put the name of the worksheet before the named range; e.g., Sheet1!myNamedRange.

- Refers To is the range the name refers to. This can also be a literal value or a formula.

Rules for Creating Names

- It can start with a letter or an underscore (_).

- The name cannot exceed 255 characters.

- Spaces are not allowed as part of a name.

- Names cannot be the same as a cell reference, such as A$35.

- You cannot use C, c, R, or r as a defined name—they are used as selection shortcuts.

Some examples of good descriptive names are as follows:

- SalesReps or sales_reps

- CompanyNames or company_names

- StudentsList or students_list

Benefits of Named Ranges

Some of the benefits of named ranges are as follows:

- Names are easier to remember when typing formulas.

- Formulas are easier to read when using named ranges.

- You can jump to a specific location easily without the need to remember the row and column address.

Excel Tables

Tables allow you to easily manage and analyze a group of related data. You can turn a range of cells into an Excel table. Every Excel table that you create is automatically named by Excel. You can change the table name to your liking. So, you can see that a table name is like a named range. Tables are a powerful but often overlooked feature of Excel.

Benefits of Using Excel Tables

Using Excel tables provides quite a few advantages, like the following:

- Excel keeps track of the range used for the table. This frees you from having to manually track row/column additions/deletions.

- Users typically face a problem when working with a large data set. The column headers tend to disappear as you scroll down the data. Tables solve this problem. When the column headers scroll off, Excel replaces the names of the worksheet columns with table headers. This will happen only when a cell in the table is selected.

- Excel tables can have a dedicated Total row, which is automatically updated as data is added/modified/deleted.

- When you enter a formula in a column of an Excel table, the formula is automatically copied throughout the column. You do not have copy and paste the formula to other cells.

- Sort and filter options are available the moment you create an Excel table.

Creating a Table

The following are the steps to create an Excel table:

1. Select a cell in the data that you wish to convert to an Excel table.

2. Select the *Table* option, as shown in Figure 5-3. The Table button is in the Insert tab.

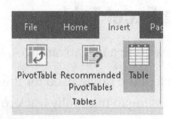

Figure 5-3. *Create a table*

3. In the Create Table dialog box, the range for your data should automatically appear. Depending on the type of data in the table, the *My table has headers* option may or may not be checked. You can adjust the range and uncheck or check the box if required. Figure 5-4 shows the Create Table dialog box. Click OK to accept changes.

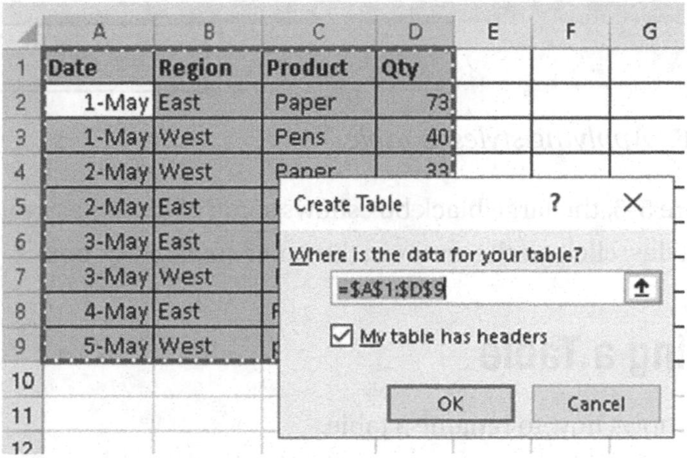

Figure 5-4. *Create Table dialog box*

Figure 5-5 shows a table after it's been created.

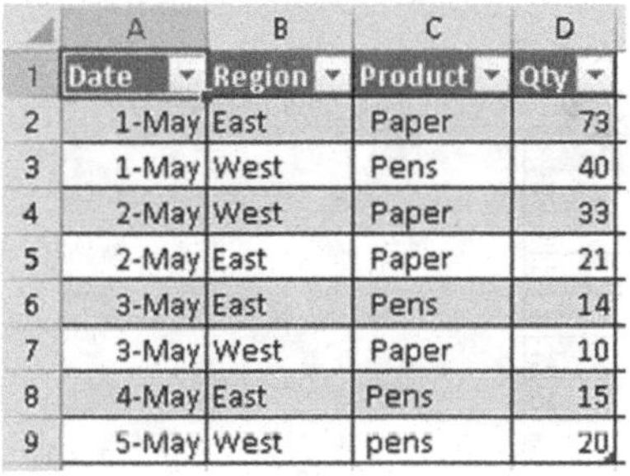

	A	B	C	D
1	Date	Region	Product	Qty
2	1-May	East	Paper	73
3	1-May	West	Pens	40
4	2-May	West	Paper	33
5	2-May	East	Paper	21
6	3-May	East	Pens	14
7	3-May	West	Paper	10
8	4-May	East	Pens	15
9	5-May	West	pens	20

Figure 5-5. *Excel table*

As you can see, the data is nicely formatted with filters automatically applied to the column headers.

Styling a Table

You can also apply formatting to the table. Figure 5-6 shows how to apply styles to format your table.

Figure 5-6. *Applying styles to table*

In Figure 5-6, the large black box shows some of the styles available. To see more styles, click on the arrow in the inner small black box.

Renaming a Table

Figure 5-7 shows how to rename a table.

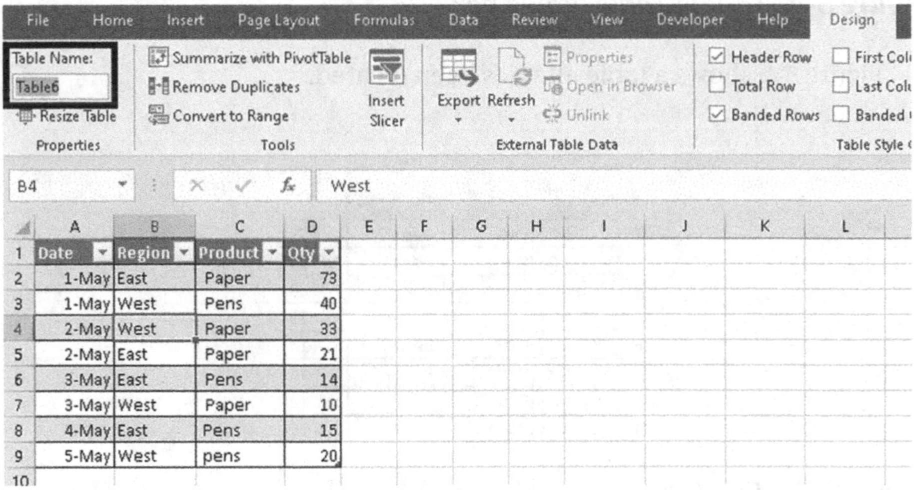

Figure 5-7. *Rename a table*

To rename a table, the steps are as follows:

1. Ensure that the active cell is in the table to be renamed.

2. Click on the Design tab in the ribbon bar.

3. By default, Excel gives a name to every table that
    you create. To change the name, click on the Table
    Name box highlighted by the black box in Figure 5-7.
    Change the table name and press the Enter key so
    that the new name is used.

Note   Table names follow the same rules as named ranges.

Adding a Reference to Another Table

Figure 5-8 shows how to refer to one table from another in a formula.

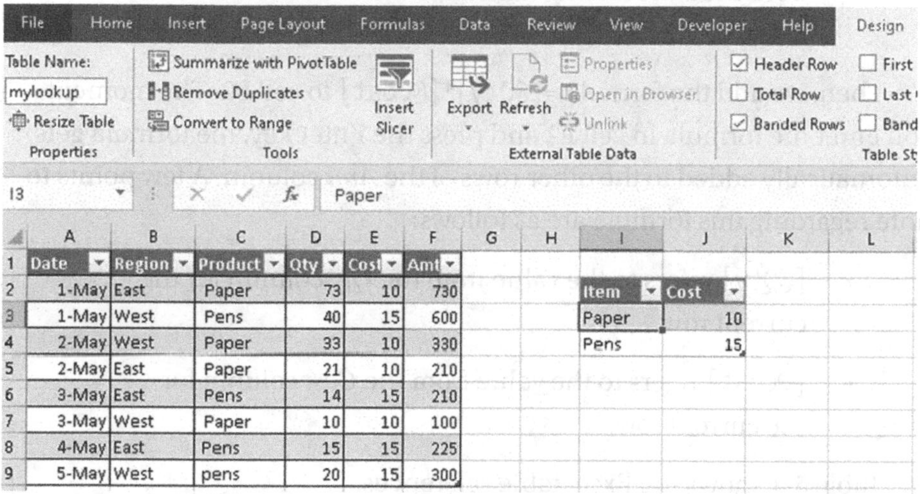

Figure 5-8. *How to refer to one table from another in a formula*

In Figure 5-8, we have created a lookup table in the cells I3 to J4. This
lookup table contains the items and their cost per unit. We have named
this lookup table *mylookup*, as can be seen in Figure 5-8.

First, we add a new column named *Cost* in column E. The moment you enter "Cost" in cell E1 and press the Enter key, the new column gets automatically added to the existing table. Similarly, add the value *Amt* in cell F1.

Next, we add the formula =VLOOKUP([@Product],mylookup,2,0) to cell E2. The moment you enter the formula in cell E2 and press the Enter key, the formula gets automatically added to the other rows of the *Cost* column. A few points to note regarding this VLOOKUP formula are as follows:

- You might be wondering what the [@Product] in the VLOOKUP formula is. Well, it refers to the value in the *Product* column for the current row.

- Similarly, for the second argument of VLOOKUP, we have used the lookup table name instead of a cell range.

Then, we add the formula =[@Qty]*[@Cost] to cell F2. The moment you enter the formula in cell F2 and press the Enter key, the formula gets automatically added to the other rows of the *Amt* column. A few points to note regarding this formula are as follows:

- [@Qty] refers to the value from the *Qty* column for the current row.

- [@Cost] refers to the value from the *Cost* column for the current row.

Table 5-1 shows the Excel table references.

Table 5-1. *Excel Table References*

Referring to	Referred in Formula as	Comments
The entire table	=Table1	We use the table name to refer to the entire table.
The current row	=Table1[@Qty]	We prefix the column name with an @ sign to indicate the current row.
Table headers	=Table1[#Headers]	This is used when you want to refer to only the table headers in your formula.

Adding a *Total* Row to the Table

Now, let us add a *Total* row to the table. Figure 5-9 shows the table with a *Total* row.

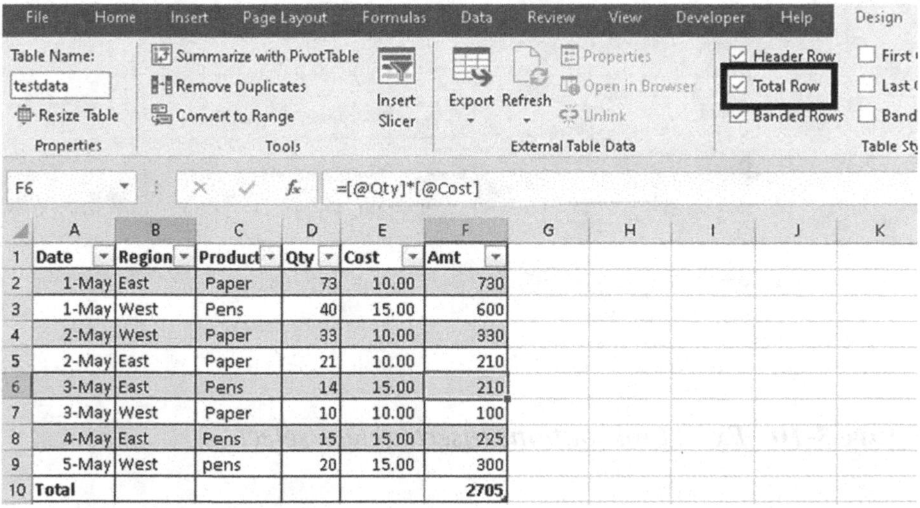

Figure 5-9. *Total row in table*

To add a *Total* row to your table, do the following:

1. Ensure that a cell in the table is selected.

2. Select the Design ribbon and then click on Total
    Row, as shown by the black box in Figure 5-9.

3. You get the total for the *Amt* column. This is the
    default behavior.

4. The formula that Excel will automatically put in cell
    F10 is =SUBTOTAL(109,[Amt]). We will look into the
    SUBTOTAL function in the chapter on aggregate
    functions.

Your table should look like the one in Figure 5-9 after adding the
Total row.

Figure 5-10 shows the options to insert/delete/select when you right-
click on a table cell. The options are pretty self-explanatory.

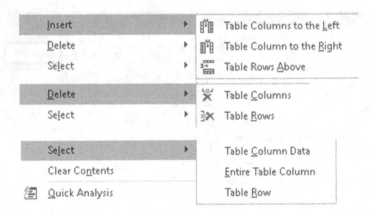

Figure 5-10. *Excel table options insert/delete/select*

Summary

To summarize, in this chapter we looked at named ranges and Excel tables. As always, I suggest you try out the examples from this chapter using your own data and also using the different options for the arguments. This will give you more clarity regarding how the functions actually work.

In the next chapter, we will look at lookup functions.

CHAPTER 6

Lookup & Reference Functions

In this chapter, we will look at some of the most commonly used lookup and reference functions in Excel.

Note In the search range argument used in this chapter, it is suggested you use absolute references. This will make it easy to copy formulas to other locations without changing the search range.

Let us now look at some of the common lookup and reference functions.

VLOOKUP Function

The VLOOKUP function is used to perform vertical lookups. Here, a value is searched for in the first column of a range, and a value in the same row from a specified column of the search range is returned. The VLOOKUP function is not case sensitive.

© Mandeep Mehta 2021
M. Mehta, *Microsoft Excel Functions Quick Reference*,
https://doi.org/10.1007/978-1-4842-6613-7_6

Limitations of VLOOKUP

- The search value should be in the first column of the search range.

- The column for return value will always be on the right.

Syntax

=VLOOKUP(*search value, search range, column number in the range from which value is to be returned, [whether to return an approximate match]*)

The VLOOKUP function takes the following arguments:

- The first argument is the value to search for. You can include wildcard characters "*" and "?" in the search value. The "*" will match any number of characters, and a "?" will match a single character.

- The second argument is the range of cells where the search is to be done. This can be a cell range, a named range in Excel or an Excel table, or the result of another formula that returns ranges, such as INDEX, OFFSET, INDIRECT, etc.

- The third argument specifies the column number in the range, starting from the first column of the search range, from which a value is to be returned.

- The fourth argument specifies whether to do an approximate match. This argument is optional.

- If the fourth argument is TRUE or 1, an approximate match is done. The value *TRUE* is used if the fourth argument is omitted. An approximate match means two values that are about the same, but not necessarily identical, should match. Some of the scenarios where *TRUE* would be used are as follows:

    - Calculating salesmen commissions

    - Calculating sales discounts

- If the fourth argument is FALSE or 0, an exact match is done.

If VLOOKUP finds a match, it returns a value. If a value is not found, it returns an error. In cases of duplicate values, VLOOKUP will return the first value that matches.

Possible Causes of Value Not Found by VLOOKUP

- The data type of the search value is not the same as the data type of the first column in the search range.

- The search value contains spaces.

Example

Figure 6-1 shows an example of the VLOOKUP function.

	A	B	C	D
1	Roll No	Name	English	Maths
2	1	Roy	25	20
3	2	Dilip	15	18
4	3	Shalu	28	27
5	4	Mary	19	21
6				
7	Name	Shalu		
8	English	28		
9	Maths	27		

Figure 6-1. *VLOOKUP function*

We have our data in cells A1 to D5. Cell B7 contains the value *Shalu*, the name of the student whose grades we are trying to find.

In cell B8, we have the function =VLOOKUP(B7,$B$1:$D$5,2,0). This will return the value *28*. This is the grade "Shalu" got in English. Let us understand this VLOOKUP function.

1. The cells from B1 to D5 specify the search range.

2. The last argument is 0, which means we want an exact match.

3. The first column of the range is the cells from B1 to B5. So, the value in cell B7 (*Shalu*) is searched for in the range B1 to B5. It is found in the fourth row of the range.

4. Since the third argument is 2, we are telling VLOOKUP to return the value at the intersection of the fourth row found in step 2 and column 2. This is cell C4.

5. So, VLOOKUP will return the value in cell C4 (*28*).

In cell B9, we have used the function =VLOOKUP(B7,$B$1:$D$5,3,0). This will return the grades for Shalu from the Math column.

Now, try to change the value in cell B7 to one of the following—*Roy*, *Dilip*, *Mary*—and see what happens.

Note   Always try to use absolute references in the second parameter of the VLOOKUP function. That way, if you copy the formula into another cell, the search range will not change.

HLOOKUP Function

The HLOOKUP function is used to perform horizontal lookups. Here, a value is searched for in the first row of a range, and a value in the same column from a specified row of the search range is returned. The HLOOKUP function is not case sensitive.

Syntax

=HLOOKUP(*search value, search range, row number in the range from which value is to be returned, [whether to return an approximate match]*)

The HLOOKUP function takes the following arguments:

- The first argument is the value to search for. You can include wildcard characters "*" and "?" in the search value. The "*" will match any number of characters, and a "?" will match a single character.

- The second argument is the range of cells where the search is to be done. This can be a cell range, a named range in Excel or an Excel table, or the result of another formula that returns ranges, such as INDEX, OFFSET, INDIRECT, etc.

- The third argument specifies the row number in the range, starting from the first row of the search range, from which the value is to be returned.

- The fourth argument specifies whether to do an approximate match. This argument is optional.

- If the fourth argument is TRUE or 1, an approximate match is done. The value *TRUE* is used if the fourth argument is omitted.

- If the fourth argument is FALSE or 0, an exact match is done.

If HLOOKUP finds a match, it returns a value. If a value is not found, it returns an error. In cases of duplicate values, HLOOKUP will return the first value that matches.

Example

Figure 6-2 shows an example of the HLOOKUP function.

▲	A	B	C	D	E
1	Roll No	1	2	3	4
2	Name	Roy	Dilip	Shalu	Mary
3	English	25	15	28	19
4	Maths	20	18	27	21
5					
6					
7	Name	Shalu			
8	English	28			
9	Maths	27			

Figure 6-2. *HLOOKUP function*

We have our data in cells A1 to E4. Cell B7 contains the value *Shalu*, the name of the student whose grades we are trying to find.

In cell B8, we have the function =HLOOKUP(B7,$B$2:$E$4,2,0). This will return the value *28*. This is the grade "Shalu" got in English. Let us understand this HLOOKUP function.

1. The cells from B2 to E4 specify the search range.

2. The last argument is 0, which means we want an exact match.

3. The first row of the range is the cells from B2 to E2. So, the value in cell B7 (*Shalu*) is searched for in the range B2 to E2. It is found in the third column of the range.

4. Since the third argument is 2, we are telling HLOOKUP to return the value at the intersection of the third column found in step 2 and row 2. This is cell D3.

5. So, HLOOKUP will return the value in cell D3 (*28*).

In cell B9, we have used the function =HLOOKUP(B7,$B$2:$E$4,3,0). This will return the grades for Shalu from the Math row.

MATCH Function

The MATCH function is used to return the position of a search value. So, if a value is searched for in a column, the MATCH function returns the row number where the search value is found. Likewise, if a value is searched for in a row, the MATCH function returns the column number where the search value is found.

Syntax

=MATCH(*search value, search range, [match type]*)

The MATCH function takes the following arguments:

- The first argument is the search value.

- The second argument is the search range. This can be a cell range, a named range or an Excel table, or the result of another formula that returns ranges, such as INDEX, OFFSET, INDIRECT, etc.

- The third argument specifies how the search should happen. The valid values are *0*, *1*, and *-1*.

- For the third argument, a value of zero (*0*) indicates an exact match should happen. This is the most frequently used value.

- For the third argument, a value of *1* finds the largest value less than or equal to the search value. The search range must be sorted in ascending order. This is the default value if match type is omitted.

- For the third argument, a value of *-1* finds the smallest value greater than or equal to the search value. The search range must be sorted in descending order.

Example

Figure 6-3 shows an example of the MATCH function.

◢	A	B	C
1	Name		Search for
2	Roy		Roy
3	Dilip		
4	Shalu		1
5	Mary		

Figure 6-3. *MATCH function*

In cell C4 we have used the function =MATCH(C2,$A$2:$A$5,0). The value returned is *1*. Here, we are asking MATCH to find the value in cell C2 (*Roy*) in the range A2 to A5. As *Roy* occurs in the first row of the search range, the value *1* is returned. If we change the function to =MATCH(C2,$A$1:$A$5,0), the value returned is *2* as now the value *Roy* occurs in the second row of the search range A1 to A5.

Note   You have to take care that you are using the correct search range, or else the results could be surprising, as we saw in the preceding example.

Figure 6-4 shows an example of the MATCH function being used with VLOOKUP.

◢	A	B	C	D
1	Roll No	Name	English	Maths
2	1	Roy	25	20
3	2	Dilip	15	18
4	3	Shalu	28	27
5	4	Mary	19	21
6				
7	Name	Shalu		
8	English	28		

Figure 6-4. *VLOOKUP with MATCH function*

In Figure 6-4, the function used in cell B8 is =VLOOKUP(B7,$B$1:$D$5, MATCH(A8,$B$1:$D$1,0),0). This function is the same as the one used in cell B8 in Figure 6-1, except for one change. For the third argument we have used the function MATCH(A8,$B$1:$D$1,0) instead of the value 2. Here, the MATCH function searches for the value from cell A8 (*English*) in cells B1 to D1. The value *English* occurs in the second column of the search range. As we want an exact match (the third argument for the MATCH function is the value 0) we get the return value 2.

Try changing the value in cell A8 to *Math* and see what value you get in cell B8.

NESTED FUNCTION

The preceding problem is an example of a nested function. A nested function is a function that contains another function as its argument. In the previous example, the MATCH function is used as the third argument of the VLOOKUP function.

INDEX Function

The INDEX function returns a cell reference at the intersection of the row number and the column number specified in the arguments from a given search range. The INDEX function has two forms: the array form and the reference form. In this book, we will be looking at the array form.

Syntax

=INDEX(*search range, row number, [column number]*)

The INDEX function takes the following arguments:

- The first argument is the search range where the search will happen.

- The second argument is the row number from which data is to be picked.

- The third argument is the column number from which data is to be picked. This argument is optional.

Note   If both row number and column number are supplied, the INDEX function returns the value in the cell at the intersection of row number and column number. It may be worth noting that if the search range is a single horizontal row, Excel will happily accept a column number instead of a row number in the second argument.

If row number is set to zero, the INDEX function will return an array of values for an entire column.

If column number is set to zero, the INDEX function returns an array of values for an entire row.

Example

Figure 6-5 shows an example of an INDEX function.

◢	A	B	C	D
1	Roll No	Name	English	Maths
2	1	Roy	25	20
3	2	Dilip	15	18
4	3	Shalu	28	27
5	4	Mary	19	21
6				
7	Name	Shalu		
8	English	28		

Figure 6-5. *INDEX function*

In cell A8 we have used the function =INDEX($A$1:$D$5,4,3). The value returned is *28*. Here, we are telling the INDEX function to return the cell in the fourth row and third column position in the range A1 to D5. This refers to cell C4. In this example, we have used fixed values for the row number and the column number. You will generally not used fixed numbers in real life. Instead, you could use the MATCH function within the INDEX function. Figure 6-6 shows an example of the MATCH function being used with the INDEX function.

◢	A	B	C	D
1	Roll No	Name	English	Maths
2	1	Roy	25	20
3	2	Dilip	15	18
4	3	Shalu	28	27
5	4	Mary	19	21
6				
7	Name	Shalu		
8	English	28		

Figure 6-6. *INDEX function with MATCH function*

In cell B8 we have used the formula =INDEX($A$1:$D$5,MATCH(B7,$B$1:$B$5,0),MATCH(A8,$A$1:$D$1,0)). Let us understand this formula:

1. The first argument to the INDEX function is the search range from A1 to D5. Note that we have used an absolute reference for the search range.

2. The second argument to the INDEX function is MATCH(B7,$B$1:$B$5,0). Here, we are telling the MATCH function to find the value in cell B7 (*Shalu*) in the range B1 to B5. This will return *4*, as the value *Shalu* occurs in the fourth row of the search range B1 to B5.

3. The third argument to the INDEX function is
    MATCH(A8,$A$1:$D$1, 0). Here, we are telling
    the MATCH function to find the value in cell A8
    (*English*) in the range A1 to D1. This will return *3*, as
    the value *English* occurs in the third column of the
    search range A1 to D1.

4. Now that we have gotten the row and column
    reference, we are telling INDEX function to return
    the cell value at the intersection of the fourth row
    and third column. This is the value in cell C4.

CHOOSE Function

The CHOOSE function is used to return a value from a list of values based
on a specified position.

Syntax

=CHOOSE(*index number, value1, [value2], [value3],.... [value254]*)

The CHOOSE function takes the following arguments:

- The first argument is the index number to be returned
  from the list of values. This argument can be a cell
  reference or a formula, or a literal value.

- Value1 to value254 is the list of values to choose from.
  Value1 is mandatory. Value2 to value254 are optional.

Example

Figure 6-7 shows an example of the CHOOSE function.

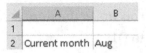

Figure 6-7. *CHOOSE function*

In cell B2 we have used the formula =CHOOSE(MONTH(TODAY()), "Jan", "Feb", "Mar", "Apr", "May", "Jun", "Jul", "Aug", "Sep", "Oct", "Nov", "Dec").

This will return the value *Aug*. Let us understand this formula:

- First the formula MONTH(TODAY()) is evaluated. Assuming today's date is in August, this will return the value *8*. This is the index number of the value that needs to be returned. Your result could vary based on your system date.

- Next, we get the eighth value from the list of values. The eighth value is the value *Aug*.

- So, the value *Aug* is returned by the formula.

FORMULATEXT Function

The FORMULATEXT function returns the formula of a specified cell in text format.

Syntax

=FORMULATEXT(cell reference)

The FORMULATEXT function expects one argument, as follows:

- The reference of the cell whose formula is to be returned in text format.

Example

Figure 6-8 shows an example of the FORMULATEXT function.

	A	B	C	D	E	F	G	H	I	J
1	Todays' date	26-08-2020								
2	Current month	Aug								
3	=CHOOSE(MONTH(B1), "Jan", "Feb", "Mar", "Apr", "May", "Jun", "Jul", "Aug", "Sep", "Oct", "Nov", "Dec")									

Figure 6-8. *FORMULATEXT function*

In Figure 6-8, in cell B2, we have used the function
=CHOOSE(MONTH(B1), "Jan", "Feb", "Mar", "Apr", "May", "Jun",
"Jul", "Aug", "Sep", "Oct", "Nov", "Dec"). In cell A3, we
have used the formula =FORMULATEXT(B2). This will return the value
=CHOOSE(MONTH(B1), "Jan", "Feb", "Mar", "Apr", "May", "Jun", "Jul",
"Aug", "Sep", "Oct", "Nov", "Dec").

ADDRESS Function

The ADDRESS function is used to create a cell reference in text format.

Syntax

=ADDRESS(row number, column number, [reference type],
[reference style], [sheet name])

The ADDRESS function takes the following arguments:

- The first argument is the row number.

- The second argument is the column number.

- The third argument specifies whether reference type is absolute or relative. This argument is optional.

- The fourth argument specifies the reference style. This argument is optional.

- The fifth argument is the sheet name to include in the address. This argument is optional. If a value is supplied for the fifth argument, it should be a text string enclosed in double quotes (""). If this argument is omitted, the current sheet name is used.

Table 6-1 shows the values that can be used for the reference-type argument and their meanings.

Table 6-1. *Reference Type*

Value for Reference Type	Description
1 or omitted	Absolute cell reference will be created like in $A$1
2	Mixed cell reference is created like A$1, where column is a relative reference and row is an absolute reference.
3	Mixed cell reference like $A1, where row is a relative reference and column is an absolute reference.
4	Relative cell reference will be created like A1

Table 6-2 shows the values that can be used for the reference-style argument and their meanings.

Table 6-2. *Reference Style*

Value for Reference Style	Description
1 or TRUE or omitted	Cell address in the A1 reference style is returned.
0 or FALSE	Cell address in the R1C1 reference style is returned.

Note About Reference Style

A1 Reference Style

This is the default method used to refer to cells. All cell addresses in the A1 reference style consist of a column letter followed by a row number. For example, to refer to a cell at the intersection of column B and row 5, we use B5.

R1C1 Reference Style

This is an alternative way to refer to cells. R1C1 cell references are displayed using row and column offset values. The following are some examples of R1C1 reference style:

- R1C1 - This is an absolute reference. It refers to the cell in the first row and first column.

- R[1]C - This refers to the cell one row below the current cell containing a formula. R[1] means one row below, C without any number means same column.

- RC[-1] - This refers to the cell one column to the left. R without a number means same row as the formula, C[-1] refers to one column to the left of the current column.

Example

Table 6-3 shows examples of the ADDRESS function.

Table 6-3. *ADDRESS Function Examples*

Formula used	Result
=ADDRESS(1,1)	$A$1
=ADDRESS(1,1,4)	A1
=ADDRESS(1,1,2)	A$1
=ADDRESS(1,1,3)	$A1
=ADDRESS(1,1,1,0)	R1C1
=ADDRESS(1,1,4,0)	R[1]C[1]
=ADDRESS(1,1,1,,"Sheet2")	Sheet2!$A$1
=ADDRESS(1,1,4,,"Sheet2")	Sheet2!A1

COLUMN Function

The COLUMN function is used to get the column number. By itself, the COLUMN function is not that useful. But when used with other functions, its usefulness increases. Some of the ways in which the COLUMN function can be used are as follows:

- Create dynamic cell address along with the ADDRESS function.

- SUM every *n*th column.

- Convert column letter to a number.

Syntax

=COLUMN([*cell reference*])

The COLUMN function takes the following argument:

- The cell reference whose column number is to be returned. This argument is optional. If this argument is not given it returns the current column number.

Example

Table 6-4 shows examples of the COLUMN function used in Figure 6-9.

Table 6-4. *COLUMN Function*

Cell Reference	Formula Used in Cell	Result
B2	=COLUMN()	The return value is *2*. Column B is the second column hence the value *2* is returned.
B3	=COLUMN(C1)	The return value is *3*. Here we have passed the cell reference "C1". As column C is the third column, the value *3* is returned.

Figure 6-9. *COLUMN function*

COLUMNS Function

The COLUMNS function returns the number of columns contained in the range passed to it.

Syntax

=COLUMNS(*cell range*)

The COLUMNS function expects only the following argument:

- The cell range whose column count is to be returned

Example

Table 6-5 shows examples of the COLUMNS function.

Table 6-5. COLUMNS Function

Formula Used	Result
=COLUMNS(A1:D5)	4
=COLUMNS(A1:A13)	1

ROW Function

The ROW function is used to return the row number. By itself, the ROW function is not that useful. But when used with other functions, its usefulness increases. Some of the ways in which the ROW function can be used are as follows:

- Create running serial number for your data.

- Used to create dynamic named ranges along with the OFFSET function.

- Create dynamic cell address along with the ADDRESS function.

Syntax

=ROW([*cell reference*])

The ROW function takes the following argument:

- The cell reference whose row number is to be returned. This argument is optional. If this argument is not given, it returns the current row number.

Example

Table 6-6 shows examples of the ROW function used in Figure 6-10.

Table 6-6. *ROW Function*

Cell Reference	Formula Used in Cell	Result
B2	=ROW()	The return value is *2*, as cell B2 is in the second row.
B3	=ROW(C1)	The return value is *1*, as cell C1 is in the first row.

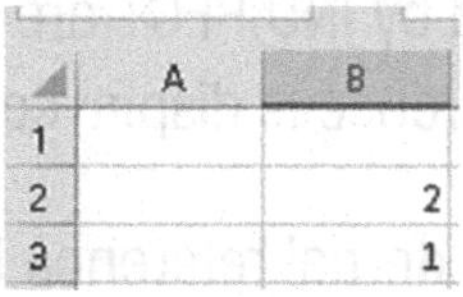

Figure 6-10. *ROW function*

ROWS Function

The ROWS function returns the number of rows contained in the range passed to it.

Syntax

```
=ROWS(cell range)
```

The ROWS function expects only the following argument:

- The cell range whose row count is to be returned

Example

Table 6-7 shows examples of the ROWS function.

Table 6-7. *ROWS Function*

Formula Used	Result
=ROWS(A1:D5)	5
=ROWS(A1:A13)	13

INDIRECT Function

The INDIRECT function is used to convert a text string into a cell reference.

Note   References created by INDIRECT are evaluated in real-time, and the content of the reference is displayed.

If the cell reference is an external reference to another workbook, the workbook must be open.

Volatile functions like INDIRECT should be avoided as much as possible unless absolutely required as they tend to make larger and more complex workbooks slow.

Syntax

```
=INDIRECT(cell reference,[reference style])
```

The INDIRECT function takes the following arguments:

- The first argument is the cell reference containing the text to be treated as cell reference.

- The second argument is used to indicate A1 or R1C1 style reference. This argument is optional. This argument can take one of two values.

  - TRUE – This is the default value. The A1 style will be used.

  - FALSE - The R1C1 style will be used.

Example

Figure 6-11 shows an example of the INDIRECT function.

◢	A	B	C
1	100	A1	100

Figure 6-11. *INDIRECT function*

In Figure 6-11, cell A1 contains the value *100*. Cell B1 contains the value *A1*. Cell C1 contains the function =INDIRECT(B1). Let us understand the steps that take place to evaluate the INDIRECT function:

1. First, the value in cell B1 is returned. This value is the text string *A1*.

2. Second, we are asking Excel to evaluate the function as =A1. This will return *100*, the value stored in A1.

95

Why Use the INDIRECT Function?

The use of the INDIRECT function might seem confusing to begin with (i.e., why not just directly use the cell reference to get the value instead of using a text string as a cell reference?). The following are a few situations where the ability to create a reference from text is useful:

- **A formula that creates a variable sheet name:**
  Figure 6-12 shows an example of a formula that creates a variable sheet name.

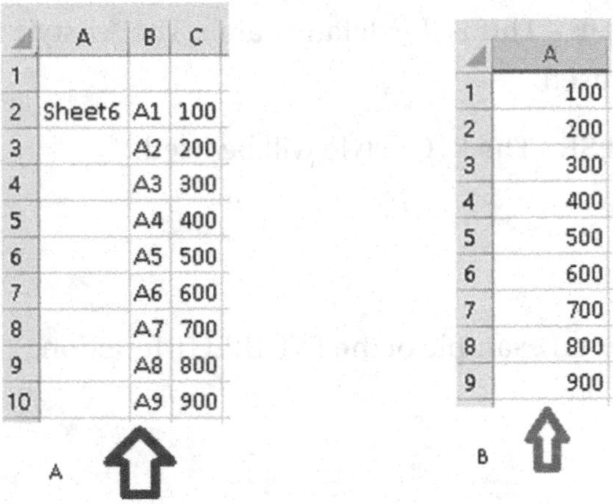

Figure 6-12. *INDIRECT function to create a variable sheet name*

In Figure 6-12, the B part indicated by the arrow is data in sheet 6. The A part indicated by the arrow is the current sheet that gets data from sheet 6 using the INDIRECT function.

Table 6-8 contains the formula used in the sheet shown by the blue arrow in Figure 6-12.

Table 6-8. *Formulas Used in the A Part of Figure 6-12*

Cell Reference	Formula Used	Description
C2	=INDIRECT ($A$2&"!"&B2)	The formula is evaluated as =INDIRECT("Sheet6!A1"). Here, we are asking for the value in cell A1 of Sheet 6.
C3	=INDIRECT ($A$2&"!"&B3)	The formula is evaluated as =INDIRECT("Sheet6!A2"). Here, we are asking for the value in cell A2 of Sheet 6.
C4	=INDIRECT ($A$2&"!"&B4)	The formula is evaluated as =INDIRECT("Sheet6!A3"). Here, we are asking for the value in cell A3 of Sheet 6.
C5	=INDIRECT ($A$2&"!"&B5)	The formula is evaluated as =INDIRECT("Sheet6!A4"). Here, we are asking for the value in cell A4 of Sheet 6.
C6	=INDIRECT ($A$2&"!"&B6)	The formula is evaluated as =INDIRECT("Sheet6!A5"). Here, we are asking for the value in cell A5 of Sheet 6.
C7	=INDIRECT ($A$2&"!"&B7)	The formula is evaluated as =INDIRECT("Sheet6!A7"). Here, we are asking for the value in cell A7 of Sheet 6.
C8	=INDIRECT ($A$2&"!"&B8)	The formula is evaluated as =INDIRECT("Sheet6!A8"). Here, we are asking for the value in cell A8 of Sheet 6.
C9	=INDIRECT ($A$2&"!"&B9)	The formula is evaluated as =INDIRECT("Sheet6!A9"). Here, we are asking for the value in cell A9 of Sheet 6.

(*continued*)

Table 6-8. (*continued*)

Cell Reference	Formula Used	Description
C10	=INDIRECT ($A$2&"!"&B10)	The formula is evaluated as =INDIRECT("Sheet6!A10"). Here, we are asking for the value in cell A10 of Sheet 6.

- **A fixed reference that will not change even when rows or columns are deleted:** The reference created by INDIRECT will not change even when cells, rows, or columns are inserted or deleted. For example, the formula =INDIRECT("A1:A5") will always refer to the first five rows of column A, even if rows in that range are deleted or inserted.

- **Create indirect references from cell values and text:** Figure 6-13 shows an example to create indirect references from cell values and text.

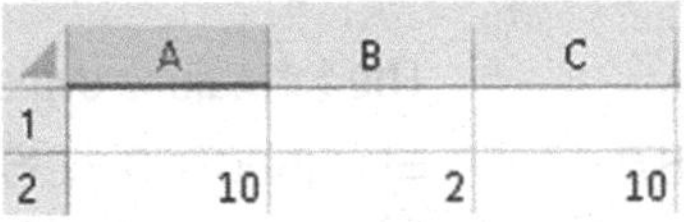

Figure 6-13. *Create indirect references from cell values and text*

In Figure 6-13, in cell C2, we have used the function =INDIRECT("A"&B2). This will be evaluated as follows:

1. "A"& B2 is evaluated to A2 as cell B2 contains the value *2*.

2. Now the function will look like =INDIRECT("A2").
   This will return the value in cell A2, which is the
   value *10*. As you can see, the value shown in cell C2
   is *10*.

Possible Issues with INDIRECT Function

The INDIRECT function returns a *#REF!* error in the following cases:

- If the cell reference is not valid

- If the cell reference refers to a range of cells beyond the
  row limit of 1,048,576 or the column limit of 16,384

- If the cell reference is of another workbook and the
  workbook is closed

OFFSET Function

The OFFSET function returns a cell range containing one or more cells
starting from a specified cell reference.

Syntax

=OFFSET(cell reference, rows, columns, [height], [width])

The OFFSET function takes the following arguments:

- The first argument can be a cell reference or a range of
  cells. This can be considered as the start position.

- The second argument is the number of rows to move
  from the start position. If this is a positive number, the
  cell moves below the start position; if the number is a
  negative number it goes above the start position.

- The third argument is the number of columns to move from the start position. If this is a positive number, the cell moves to the right of the start position; if the number is a negative number it moves to the left of the start position.

- The fourth argument is the height, in number of rows, of the returned reference. This argument is optional.

- The fifth argument is the width, in number of columns, of the returned reference. This argument is optional.

Note The height and width arguments should always be a positive number. If either of the arguments is omitted, then the height and/or width of the start position is used.

Example

Figure 6-14 shows some examples of the OFFSET function.

◢	A	B	C	D	E	F	G	H	I
1									
2		Sales	Jan	Feb	Mar	Apr	May	Jun	Total
3		North	120	230	170	240	200	170	1130
4		East	220	130	140	240	120	120	970
5		West	150	170	240	140	210	150	1060
6		South	180	110	170	130	140	120	850
7		Total	670	640	720	750	670	560	4010
8									
9				170	West Sales in Feb				
10				670	Sales in Jan				
11				1130	North Sales in 1st 6 months				
12				1980	Sales in 2nd quarter				

Figure 6-14. *OFFSET function*

In Figure 6-14, we have sales data in cells B2 to I7. Cells C2 to H2 contain the month. Cells B3 to B6 contain the regions. Cells C3 to H6 contain the data month-wise and region-wise. Cells I3 to I7 and C7 to H7 contain the totals.

In cell C9 we have the function =OFFSET(B2, 3,2). This will return the value *170*, West sales in Feb. Let us see how this works. Starting from B2 we go three rows down, which takes us to cell B5. From here we go two columns to the right, finally taking us to cell D5, whose value, *170*, is returned.

In cell C10 we have the function =SUM(OFFSET(B2, 1,1,4)). This gives us *670*, the sum of sales in Jan for all regions. The formula works as follows:

=SUM(OFFSET(B2, 1,1,4)) ➔ =SUM(C3:C6) ➔
=SUM({120;220;150;180})) ➔ 670

In cell C11 we have used the function =SUM(OFFSET(B2,1,1,1,6)). This will give us the value *1130*, the sum of all sales for the North region in C3 to H3. The formula works as follows:

=SUM(OFFSET(B2,1,1,1,6)) ➔ SUM(C3:H3) ➔
=SUM({120,230,170,240,200,170}) ➔ 1130

In cell C12 we have used the function =SUM(OFFSET(B2, 1,4, 4,3)). This will give the value *1590*, the sum of sales in the second quarter for all regions. The formula works as follows:

=SUM(OFFSET(B2, 1,4, 4,3)) ➔ SUM(F3:H6) ➔=SUM({240,200,170;240, 120,120;140,210,150;130, 140, 120}) ➔ 1980

Things to remember while using the OFFSET function:

- Volatile functions like OFFSET should be avoided as much as possible unless it is absolutely required as they tend to make larger and more complex workbooks slow.

- As references returned are dynamic, complex, and big, Excel formulas can be quite tricky to debug.

- The OFFSET function is useful when trying to create dynamic ranges.

Summary

To summarize, in this chapter we looked at some of the lookup and reference functions provided by Excel. As always, I suggest you try out the examples from this chapter using your own data and also using the different options for the arguments. This will give you more clarity regarding how the functions actually work.

In the next chapter, we will look at aggregate functions provided by Excel.

CHAPTER 7

Aggregate Functions

In this chapter, we will look into aggregate functions, which are generally used to do the following:

- Sum values

- Count values

- Average values

We will begin with functions that help do summations.

SUM Function

The SUM function is used to sum one or more numbers in a range of cells or literal values.

Syntax

=SUM(*value1*, [*value2*], ...)

The SUM function can take up to 255 arguments, as follows:

- The first argument is mandatory. The remaining arguments are optional.

- The arguments supplied to the SUM function can be a single cell reference, a cell range, or a literal numeric value.

© Mandeep Mehta 2021
M. Mehta, *Microsoft Excel Functions Quick Reference*,
https://doi.org/10.1007/978-1-4842-6613-7_7

Example

Figure 7-1 shows an example of the SUM function.

	A	B	C
1			
2	**Item**	**Month**	**Qty**
3	Shirts	Jan	500
4	Shirts	Feb	400
5	Shirts	Mar	600
6			1500

Figure 7-1. *SUM function*

In Figure 7-1, we see the sales of shirts in the months of January, February, and March. In cell C6, we have used the function `=SUM(C3:C5)`. This will sum the values in cells C3 to C5, getting the value *1,500*.

SUMIF Function

The SUMIF function is used to sum values based on a condition.

Syntax

`=SUMIF(`*`Search range, criteria, sum range`*`)`

The SUMIF function takes the following arguments:

- The first argument is the search range whose cells will be evaluated.
- The second argument is the criteria used to evaluate the cells in the search range. You can use wildcards in the criteria. A question mark (?) is used to match any single character, while an asterisk (*) is used to match any number of characters.

- The third argument is the range that should be used to sum the values.

Note   Criteria that includes text or logical or mathematical operators must be enclosed in double quotation marks (").

Logical Operators

A logical operator is used to compare two values. The result of the comparison in any case can only be either *TRUE* or *FALSE*.

Table 7-1 shows how logical operators work.

Table 7-1. *Logical Operators*

Operator	Condition	Formula Example	Description
=	Equal to	=A1=B1	The formula will return *TRUE* if a value in cell A1 is equal to the value in cell B1; else it will return *FALSE*.
	Not equal to	=A1<>B1	The formula will return *TRUE* if a value in cell A1 is not equal to the value in cell B1; else it will return *FALSE*.
>	Greater than	=A1>B1	The formula will return *TRUE* if a value in cell A1 is greater than a value in cell B1; else it will return *FALSE*.
<	Less than	=A1<B1	The formula will return *TRUE* if a value in cell A1 is less than in cell B1; else it will return *FALSE*.

(continued)

105

Table 7-1. (*continued*)

Operator	Condition	Formula Example	Description
>=	Greater than or equal to	=A1>=B1	The formula will return *TRUE* if the value in cell A1 is greater than or equal to the value in cell B1; else it will return *FALSE*.
<=	Less than or equal to	=A1<=B1	The formula will return *TRUE* if the value in cell A1 is less than or equal to the value in cell B1; else it will return *FALSE*.

Mathematical Operators

Table 7-2 shows the mathematical operators used in Excel.

Table 7-2. *Mathematical Operators*

Mathematical Operator	Symbol	Meaning
Addition	+	This is used to add two numbers.
Subtraction	-	This is used to subtract one number from another. For example, 3 - 1. Here, we want to subtract the number 1 from the number 3.
Multiplication	*	This is used to multiply two numbers.
Division	/	This is used to divide one number by another. For example, 3/1. Here, we want to divide the number 3 by the number 1.
Exponentiation	^	This is used to find the power of a number. For example, 5^2 will return the value 25. Here, are trying to calculate the square of 5.

Mathematical operators can be used with

- numeric values;

- cell references containing numeric values; and

- formulas that evaluate to numeric values.

Excel will evaluate a formula containing logical and mathematical operators in the following order:

1. First, any expressions in parentheses will evaluated.

2. Next, exponentiation operations will be carried out.

3. Then, multiplication and division are evaluated.

4. Next, addition and subtraction are evaluated.

5. Finally, logical operators are evaluated.

Example

Figure 7-2 shows an example of the SUMIF function.

	A	B	C	D	E
1					
2	Item	Month	Qty		
3	Shirts	Jan	500		Jan Sales
4	Pants	Jan	230		1030
5	Track Pants	Jan	100		
6	Suits	Jan	50		
7	T Shirts	Jan	150		
8	Shirts	Feb	500		
9	Pants	Feb	230		
10	Track Pants	Feb	100		
11	Suits	Feb	50		
12	T Shirts	Feb	150		
13	Shirts	Mar	500		
14	Pants	Mar	230		
15	Track Pants	Mar	100		
16	Suits	Mar	50		
17	T Shirts	Mar	150		

Figure 7-2. *SUMIF function*

In Figure 7-2, we have created a table from the cell range A2 to C17. In cell E3, we have used the function =SUMIF(Table1[Month], "Jan", Table1[Qty]). This will give us the value *1,030*, the sales quantity in January. Let us understand this function. Here, we are asking Excel to sum all the values in the *Qty* column where the *Month* column has the value *Jan*. As can be seen, the black boxes identify the cells that are considered.

If we use the function =SUMIF(Table1[Item], "*Pants", Table1[Qty]), we get the sum of *Qty* sold for *Pants* and *Track Pants* for the months *Jan* to *Mar*. As we have used the wildcard character '*' for the criteria, the function will consider both *Pants* and *Track Pants*.

SUMIFS Function

The SUMIFS function is used to sum values based on one or more conditions.

Syntax

=SUMIFS(*sum range, criteria range1, criteria1,[criteria range2], [criteria2], ...*)

The SUMIFS function takes the following arguments:

- The first argument is the range from which the values are to be summed.

- The second argument is the criteria range that will be checked against the given criteria. You can use wildcards in the criteria. A question mark (?) is used to match any single character, while an asterisk (*) is used to match any number of characters.

Note   Criteria that includes text or logical or mathematical operators must be enclosed in double quotation marks (").

- The third argument is the criteria to be checked for.

A total of 127 pairs of criteria ranges and criteria can be used in the SUMIFS function.

Example

Figure 7-3 shows an example of the SUMIFS function.

	A	B	C	D	E	F
1						
2	Item ▼	Month ▼	Qty ▼			
3	Shirts	Jan	500		500	Sales of Shirts in Jan
4	Pants	Jan	230			
5	Track Pants	Jan	100			
6	Suits	Jan	50			
7	T Shirts	Jan	150			
8	Shirts	Feb	500			
9	Pants	Feb	230			
10	Track Pants	Feb	100			
11	Suits	Feb	50			
12	T Shirts	Feb	150			
13	Shirts	Mar	500			
14	Pants	Mar	230			
15	Track Pants	Mar	100			
16	Suits	Mar	50			
17	T Shirts	Mar	150			

Figure 7-3. *SUMIFS function*

In Figure 7-3, we have created a table from the cell range A2 to C17. In cell E3 we have used the function =SUMIFS(Table1[Qty],Table1[Item], "Shirts", Table1[Month], "Jan"). This will give the value *500*. Here, we are asking SUMIFS to return the sum of rows where the *Item* column has the value *Shirts* and the value in the *Month* column is *Jan*.

If we use the formula =SUM(SUMIFS(Table1[Qty],Table1[Item], "Shirts", Table1[Month], {"Jan", "Feb"})), we get the value *1000*, which is the sum of shirts sold in January and February. Let us see how this formula works:

1. First, the inner formula SUMIFS(Table1[Qty],Tab le1[Item], "Shirts", Table1[Month], {"Jan", "Feb"}) is evaluated. This gives the values *{500,500}*, which are given to the outer SUM function.

2. Next, the outer SUM function is evaluated as SUM({500,500}). This will return the value *1,000*.

This example could be written as follows:

```
SUMIFS(Table1[Qty],Table1[Item], "Shirts", Table1[Month],
"Jan") + SUMIFS(Table1[Qty],Table1[Item], "Shirts",
Table1[Month],"Feb")
```

This formula is longer but it is easier to understand and debug. We can clearly see that first we sum shirts sold in January. To this we add the shirts sold in February.

SUMPRODUCT Function

The SUMPRODUCT function returns the sum of the products of arrays.

Syntax

```
=SUMPRODUCT(array1, [array2], [array3]...)
```

The SUMPRODUCT can take up to 255 arrays. The first argument is mandatory; the others are optional.

Note   The following points should be kept in mind while using the SUMPRODUCT function:

- Wildcard characters are not supported by the SUMPRODUCT function.

- All the arrays that are used in a SUMPRODUCT formula must have the same number of rows and columns.

- If an array argument is a logical test, then it will result in *TRUE* and *FALSE* values. You will need to use the double unary operator (--) or any form of multiplication (e.g., multiply by 1) to convert the *TRUE/FALSE* values to *1* and *0*.

- If any array argument contains non-numeric values, the non-numeric values will be treated as zeros.

Example

Figure 7-4 shows an example of the SUMPRODUCT function.

	A	B	C	D	E
1					
2	Item	Month	Qty		
3	Shirts	Jan	500		500
4	Pants	Jan	230		
5	Track Pants	Jan	100		
6	Suits	Jan	50		
7	T Shirts	Jan	150		
8	Shirts	Feb	500		
9	Pants	Feb	230		
10	Track Pants	Feb	100		
11	Suits	Feb	50		
12	T Shirts	Feb	150		
13	Shirts	Mar	500		
14	Pants	Mar	230		
15	Track Pants	Mar	100		
16	Suits	Mar	50		
17	T Shirts	Mar	150		

Figure 7-4. *SUMPRODUCT function*

In Figure 7-4, we have created a table from the cell range A2 to C17. In cell E3 we have used the function =SUMPRODUCT(--(Table1[Month]="Jan"), --(Table1[Item]="Shirts"), Table1[Qty]). Here, we are asking for the quantity sold in January for shirts. This will return the value *500*. Let us understand this function:

1. The first argument --(Table1[Month]="Jan") is evaluated to *{1;1;1;1;1;0;0;0;0;0;0;0;0;0;0}*. If we did not use the double unary operator (--), then the first argument would be evaluated to *{TRUE;TRUE;TRUE ;TRUE;TRUE;FALSE;FALSE;FALSE;FALSE;FALSE;FA LSE;FALSE;FALSE;FALSE;FALSE}*.

2. The second argument --(Table1[Item]="Shirts") is evaluated to *{1;0;0;0;1;0;0;0;0;1;0;0;0;0}*.

3. The third argument Table1[Qty] is evaluated to *{500;230;100;50;150;500;230;100;50;150;500;230; 100;50;150}*.

4. Next, each of the corresponding values is multiplied as given in Table 7-3.

Table 7-3. *Argument Values After They Are Converted*

1st Argument A	2nd Argument B	3rd Argument C	Product of the 3 Argument Values A*B*C
1	1	500	500
1	0	230	0
1	0	100	0
1	0	50	0
1	0	150	0

(*continued*)

Table 7-3. (*continued*)

1st Argument A	2nd Argument B	3rd Argument C	Product of the 3 Argument Values A*B*C
0	1	500	0
0	0	230	0
0	0	100	0
0	0	50	0
0	0	150	0
0	1	500	0
0	0	230	0
0	0	100	0
0	0	50	0
0	0	150	0
0	0	500	0

5. Finally, the SUMPRODUCT function will return
    the total sum for the product column in Table 7-3,
    which is the value *500*.

The formula (=SUMPRODUCT(--(Table1[Month]="Jan"),
--(Table1[Item]="Shirts"), Table1[Qty])) can also be written in
either of the following two ways:

- =SUMPRODUCT((Table1[Month]="Jan") * 1,
  (Table1[Item]="Shirts") * 1, Table1[Qty]) – In
  this approach we are multiplying the arguments by 1
  instead of using the double unary operator. The idea
  behind multiplying is to convert the *TRUE/FALSE*
  values to *1* and *0*.

- =SUMPRODUCT((Table1[Month]="Jan") *
  (Table1[Item]="Shirts") * Table1[Qty]) - In this
  approach we are multiplying all the arguments.

Both these variations will return the value *500*.

If we use the formula =SUMPRODUCT(--(Table1[Month]="Jan"),
Table1[Qty]), we will get the quantity sold in January, which is *1,030*. This
formula can also be written in either of the following two ways:

- =SUMPRODUCT((Table1[Month]="Jan") * 1,
  Table1[Qty])

- =SUMPRODUCT((Table1[Month]="Jan") *
  Table1[Qty])

Both variations will return the value *1,030*.

Now let us look at a formula to find out the sales where the month
is *Jan* and the item is either *Shirts* or *Pants*. The formula will be =SUM
PRODUCT((Table1[Month]="Jan") * ((Table1[Item]="Shirts") +
(Table1[Item]="Pants")) *Table1[Qty]). This will return the value *730*.

The new thing in this formula is the part (Table1[Item]="Shirts")
+ (Table1[Item]="Pants"). The '+' symbol tells Excel to return a *TRUE*
value if any of the conditions in a given expression evaluates to *TRUE*.
Here, we are telling Excel to return *TRUE* if the item is either *Shirts* or *Pants*
while evaluating the formula.

Now we will look into functions that allow us to count.

For these examples, we have created a named range *cnt* that refers to
cells A2 to A16 in Figure 7-5.

⊿	A	B	C	D
1				
2	12		COUNT	6
3	5		COUNTA	12
4			COUNTBLANK	3
5	abc		COUNTIF	3
6	23		cells containing text	3
7	65			
8	xyz			
9	pqr			
10	41			
11	TRUE			
12	FALSE			
13	33			
14	#DIV/0!			
15				
16				

Figure 7-5. *Examples of the Functions COUNT, COUNTA, COUNTBLANK, COUNTIF*

COUNT Function

The COUNT function is used to count the number of cells in a range with numeric values.

Syntax

=COUNT(*value1*, [*value2*], ...)

The COUNT function can take up to 255 arguments:

- The first argument *value1* is mandatory. The remaining arguments are optional.

- The arguments supplied to the COUNT function can be a single cell reference or a cell range.

Example

In cell D2 we have used the function = COUNT(cnt). This will return the value *6*. As you can see in Figure 7-5, there are six cells that have numeric values (cells A2, A3, A6, A7, A10, A13).

COUNTA Function

The COUNTA function is used to count the number of cells in a range that are not empty.

Syntax

=COUNTA(value1, [value2], ...)

The COUNTA function can take up to 255 arguments.:

- The first argument *value1* is mandatory. The remaining arguments are optional.

- The arguments supplied to the COUNTA function can be a single cell reference or a cell range.

Example

In Figure 7-5, in cell D3, we have used the function =COUNTA(cnt). This will return the value *12*, which is the number of cells in the name range *cnt* that are not empty. As you can see in Figure 7-5, except for cells A4, A15, and A16, all cells in the named range *cnt* have values.

COUNTBLANK Function

The COUNTBLANK function is used to count the number of cells in a range that are empty.

Syntax

=COUNTBLANK(value1, [value2], ...)

    The COUNTBLANK function can take up to 255 arguments:

- The first argument *value1* is mandatory. The remaining arguments are optional.

- The arguments supplied to the COUNTBLANK function can be a single cell reference or a cell range.

Example

In Figure 7-5, in cell D3, we have used the function =COUNTBLANK(cnt). This will return the value *3*, which is the number of cells in the name range *cnt* that are empty. As you can see in Figure 7-5, cells A4, A15, and A16 in the named range *cnt* are empty.

COUNTIF Function

The COUNTIF function is used to return a count of non-blank cells in a range based on a condition.

Syntax

=COUNTIF(*range, criteria*)

The COUNTIF function expects two arguments:

- The first argument is a range to count cells in.

- The second argument is the criteria used for counting cells. You can use wildcards in the criteria. A question mark (?) is used to match any single character, while an asterisk (*) is used to match any number of characters.

Note   Criteria that includes text or logical or mathematical operators must be enclosed in double quotation marks (").

Example

In Figure 7-5, in cell D5, we have used the function =COUNTIF(cnt, ">25"). This will return the value *3*. Here, we are asking to return a count of numbers whose value is greater than 25 from the cell range *cnt*. Since there are three numbers greater than 25 (65, 41, 33), the value returned is *3*.

In Figure 7-5, in cell D6, we have used the function =COUNTIF(cnt, "*"). This will return a count of cells containing text from the named range *cnt*. This formula will ignore all cells with dates, numbers, and Boolean values. To count all non-blank cells in the named range *cnt*, we will use the formula =COUNTIF(cnt,"<>").

COUNTIFS Function

The COUNTIFS function is used to return a count of non-blank cells in a range based on one or more conditions.

Syntax

`=COUNTIFS(range, criteria)`

The COUNTIFS function takes the following arguments:

- The first argument is a range to count cells in.

- The second argument is the criteria used for counting cells. You can use wildcards in the criteria. A question mark (?) is used to match any single character, while an asterisk (*) is used to match any number of characters.

Note   Criteria that includes text or logical or mathematical operators must be enclosed in double quotation marks (").

Example

Figure 7-6 shows an example of the COUNTIFS function.

▲	A	B	C	D	E
1	Name ▼	Gender ▼	Subject ▼	Score ▼	
2	Divya	Female	Maths	50	
3	Divya	Female	English	85	
4	Divya	Female	Science	77	
5	Lewis	Male	Maths	50	
6	Lewis	Male	English	73	
7	Lewis	Male	Science	83	
8	Roby	Male	Maths	72	
9	Roby	Male	English	71	
10	Roby	Male	Science	70	
11	Sandra	Female	Maths	80	
12	Sandra	Female	English	51	
13	Sandra	Female	Science	89	
14					
15	5	How many Male test scores were greater than 60			
16	3	How many Maths tests scores were less than 80			

Figure 7-6. *COUNTIFS function*

In Figure 7-6, in cell A15, we are trying to find out how many male test scores were greater than 60. The formula we have used in cell A15 is =COUNTIFS(student[Gender], "Male", student[Score], ">60"). Here, we are saying to get the count of all male students who have gotten more than 60, irrespective of the subject. The value returned is 5.

In Figure 7-6, in cell A16, we are trying to find out how many math test scores were less than 80. The formula we have used in cell A16 is =COUNTIFS(student[Subject], "Maths", student[Score], "<80"). Here, we are saying to get the count of all students who have gotten less than 80 in math. The value returned is 3.

Next, we will look into functions that allow us to perform averages.

Figure 7-7 shows examples of the AVERAGE, AVERAGEIF, and AVERAGEIFS functions.

▲	A	B	C	D
1				
2	Product ▼	Month ▼	Sales Amount ▼	
3	Pen	Jan	200	
4	Pencil	Jan	100	
5	Eraser	Jan	300	
6	Ruler	Jan	50	
7	Pen	Feb	300	
8	Pencil	Feb	50	
9	Eraser	Feb	200	
10	Ruler	Feb	100	
11	Pen	Mar	50	
12	Pencil	Mar	300	
13	Eraser	Mar	50	
14	Ruler	Mar	200	
15				
16				
17			158.333	Avg Sales for the first quarter
18			162.5	Avg sales for Jan
19			175	Avg sales of Mar for Pen and Pencil

Figure 7-7. *Averaging functions*

AVERAGE Function

The AVERAGE function is used to perform the average of numbers in a given range.

Syntax

=AVERAGE(*value1*, [*value2*], ...)

The AVERAGE function can take up to 255 arguments:

- The first argument *value1* is mandatory. The remaining arguments are optional.

- The arguments supplied to the AVERAGE function can be a single cell reference or a cell range or literal values.

Note   If the cell range contains cells with non-numeric data, these cells are ignored for calculating the average. So, if your cell range contains non-numeric data, the AVERAGE function could give a result other than what you expect.

Example

In Figure 7-7, we have converted the cell range A2 to C14 into a table named *mydata*. In cell B17 we are trying to get the average sales for the first quarter. The formula we have used in cell B17 is =AVERAGE(mydata[Sales Amount]). This will return the value *158.333*. Here, we are finding the average of all sales for the months January to March.

AVERAGEIF Function

The AVERAGEIF function is used to find the average of values based on a condition.

Syntax

=AVERAGEIF (*search range, criteria, [average range]*)

The AVERAGEIF function takes the following arguments:

- The first argument is the search range in which the cells will be evaluated.

- The second argument is the criteria used to evaluate the cells in the search range. You can use wildcards in the criteria. A question mark (?) is used to match any single character, while an asterisk (*) is used to match any number of characters.

- The third argument is the range that should be used to average the values. This argument is optional. If this argument is omitted, the average of the cells in the search range will be done.

Example

In Figure 7-7, in cell B18, we have used the formula =AVERAGEIF(mydata[Month],"Jan", mydata[Sales Amount]). Here, we are trying to find the average of all sales for the month of January. The value returned by the formula is *162.5*.

AVERAGEIFS Function

The AVERAGEIFS function is used to find the average of values based on one or more conditions.

Syntax

=AVERAGEIFS (*average range, criteria range1, criteria1,[criteria range2], [criteria2], ...*)

The AVERAGEIFS function takes the following arguments:

- The first argument is the range for which the values are to be averaged.

- The second argument is the criteria range that will be checked against the given criteria. You can use wildcards in the criteria. A question mark (?) is used to match any single character, while an asterisk (*) is used to match any number of characters.

- The third argument is the criteria to be checked for.

A total of 127 pairs of criteria range and criteria can be used in the AVERAGEIFS function.

Example

In Figure 7-7, in cell B19, we have used the formula =AVERAGEIFS(mydata[Sales Amount], mydata[Product], "Pe*", mydata[Month], "Mar"). Here, we are trying to find the average of all sales for *Pen* and *Pencil* (observe that we have used the wildcard pattern for the criteria) for the month of *Mar*. The value returned by the formula is *175*.

Now let us look at some aggregate functions that cannot be classified under summation, counting, or averaging.

124

SUBTOTAL Function

The SUBTOTAL function performs the aggregation of a range of cells. It is generally used when you want to exclude filtered or hidden rows. It is widely used in Excel tables.

Syntax

=SUBTOTAL(*function number, ref1, [ref2],...[ref254]*)

The SUBTOTAL function can take up to 255 arguments. The first two arguments are mandatory, as follows:

- The first argument is the function number that specifies what kind of aggregation should happen. Table 7-4 shows the function numbers and the operations they perform.

- The second argument is the cell range or a named range on which to perform the function specified in the first argument.

- Ref2 to Ref254 also refer to the cell range or a named range on which to perform the function specified in the first argument. These arguments are optional.

Table 7-4. *Function Numbers Used in SUBTOTAL Function*

Function Name	Function Number That Will Include Hidden Rows	Function Number That Will Ignore Hidden Rows
AVERAGE	1	101
COUNT	2	102
COUNTA	3	103

(*continued*)

Table 7-4. (*continued*)

Function Name	Function Number That Will Include Hidden Rows	Function Number That Will Ignore Hidden Rows
MAX	4	104
MIN	5	105
PRODUCT	6	106
STDEV	7	107
STDEVP	8	108
SUM	9	109
VAR	10	110
VARP	11	101

Note   SUBTOTAL will always ignore values in cells that are hidden using a filter.

Example

Figure 7-8 shows an example of the SUBTOTAL function.

▲	A	B	C
1	Item ▼	Month ▼	Qty ▼
2	Shirts	Jan	500
3	Pants	Jan	230
4	Track Pants	Jan	100
5	Suits	Jan	50
6	T Shirts	Jan	150
7	Shirts	Feb	500
8	Pants	Feb	230
9	Track Pants	Feb	100
10	Suits	Feb	50
11	T Shirts	Feb	150
12	Shirts	Mar	500
13	Pants	Mar	230
14	Track Pants	Mar	100
15	Suits	Mar	50
16	T Shirts	Mar	150
17	Total		3090

Figure 7-8. *SUBTOTAL function*

In Figure 7-8, the function used in cell C17 is =SUBTOTAL(109,[Qty]). In this function, we have used the value *109* for the first argument. If you refer to Table 7-4, you'll see that the function number 109 performs a SUM operation while ignoring hidden rows.

Let us now hide the rows for January. Figure 7-9 shows how the *Total* row will change when we hide the rows for *Jan*.

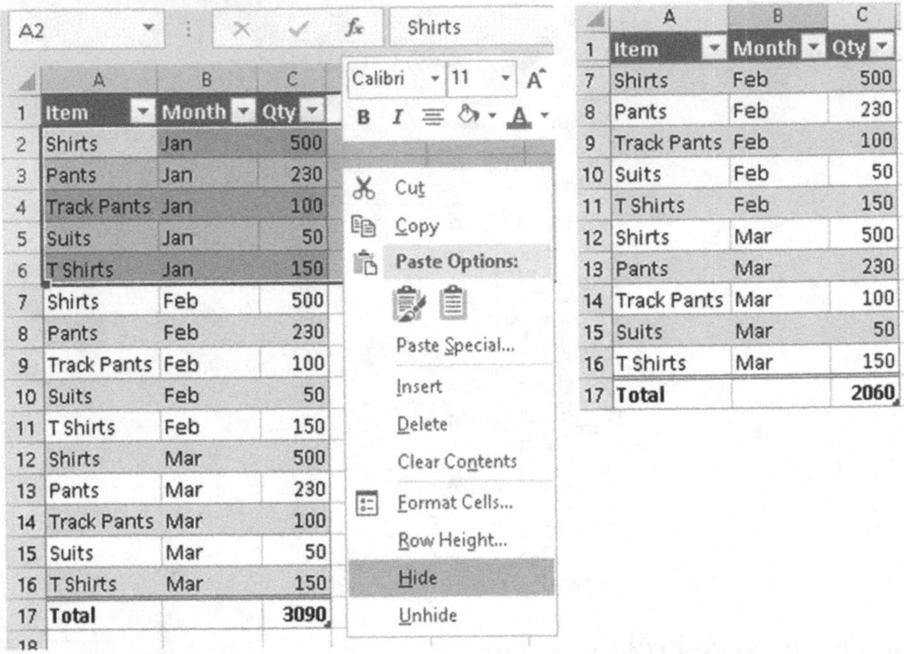

Figure 7-9. *SUBTOTAL function with hidden rows*

As you can see in Figure 7-9, the *Total Qty* value was *3,090* before the *Jan* rows were hidden. After the *Jan* rows are hidden, the *Total Qty* changes to the value *2,060*.

Now, unhide the rows for *Jan* and apply a filter to show only the months of January and February. Figure 7-10 shows an example of the SUBTOTAL function after filtering rows.

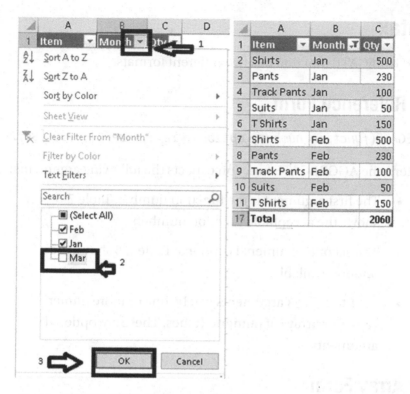

Figure 7-10. *SUBTOTAL function with filtered rows*

In Figure 7-10, the image on the left shows the steps to apply the filter to filter out *Mar*. The image on the right shows how the table will look after applying the filter.

AGGREGATE Function

The AGGREGATE function is very similar to the SUBTOTAL function, but has a few more features. The AGGREGATE function also performs an aggregation of a range of cells.

Syntax

The AGGREGATE function has two different formats.

The Reference Form

=AGGEGATE(*function number, options, ref1, [ref2], ... [ref253]*)

Here, the AGGREGATE function expects the following arguments:

- The first argument is the function number. Table 7-5 shows the acceptable function numbers.

- The second argument is options. Table 7-6 shows the options available.

- Ref1 to ref253 arguments can be one or more numeric values or arrays of numeric values. These are optional arguments.

The Array Form

=AGGREGATE(*function number, options, array, [k]*)

Here, the AGGREGATE function expects four arguments, as follows:

- The first argument is the function number. Table 7-5 shows the acceptable function numbers.

- The second argument is options. Table 7-6 shows the options available.

- The third argument is the range of cells on which the specified function is to be performed.

- The fourth argument is optional. It must be specified for the *Large, Small, Percentile,* and *Quartile* functions.

Table 7-5. *Function Numbers*
for AGGREGATE Function

Function Number	Function
1	AVERAGE
2	COUNT
3	COUNTA
4	MAX
5	MIN
6	PRODUCT
7	STDEV.S
8	STDEV.P
9	SUM
10	VAR.S
11	VAR.P
12	MEDIAN
13	MODE.SNGL
14	LARGE
15	SMALL
16	PERCENTILE. INC
17	QUARTILE.INC
18	PERCENTILE. EXC
19	QUARTILE.EXC

Table 7-6. *Options for the AGGREGATE Function*

Option	Behavior
0 or omitted	Nested SUBTOTAL and AGGREGATE functions are ignored.
1	Hidden rows, nested SUBTOTAL and AGGREGATE functions are ignored.
2	Error values, nested SUBTOTAL and AGGREGATE functions are ignored.
3	Hidden rows, error values, nested SUBTOTAL and AGGREGATE functions are ignored.
4	Nothing is ignored.
5	Hidden rows are ignored.
6	Error values are ignored.
7	Hidden rows and error values are ignored.

Example

Figure 7-11 shows some examples of the AGGREGATE functions.

⟋	A	B	C
1	49		
2	57		90
3	66		66
4	#NUM!		#VALUE!
5	66		
6	69		
7	74		
8	90		
9	53		
10	65		
11	#DIV/0!		

Figure 7-11. *AGGREGATE functions*

Table 7-7 shows the formulas used in the cells in column C in Figure 7-11.

Table 7-7. *Formulas Used in Column C in Figure 7-11*

Cell Reference	Formula Used	Description
C2	=AGGREGATE (4, 6, A1:A11)	This will calculate the maximum value while ignoring error values.
C3	=AGGREGATE (14, 6, A1:A11, 4)	This will calculate the fourth-largest value while ignoring error values.
C4	=AGGREGATE (15, 6, A1:A11)	This will return the *#VALUE!* error, Here, we are trying to get the smallest value; however, we have not given the fourth argument indicating which smallest number to return.

MAX Function

Th MAX function is used to find the maximum number from a set of numbers.

Syntax

=MAX(num1, [*num2,* ...*num255*])

The MAX function takes the following arguments:

- The first argument is a number, reference to cell with numeric value, or a cell range that contains numeric values.

- The arguments num2 to num255 are optional. They can take a number, reference to cell with numeric value, or a cell range that contains numeric values.

133

Example

Figure 7-12 shows an example of the MAX and MIN functions. We will see the MIN function next.

	A	B	C
1	MAX		MIN
2	98		77
3	47		86
4	98		39
5	100		65
6	72		50
7	67		23
8	18		70
9	37		24
10	8		44
11	77		32
12	37		26
13			
14	100		23

Figure 7-12. *MAX and MIN functions*

In Figure 7-12, in cell A14, we have used the function =MAX(A2:A12). This will find the maximum number in the cell range A2 to A12. Since 100 is the maximum number, the function returns the value *100*.

MIN Function

Th MIN function is used to find the minimum number from a set of numbers.

Syntax

=MIN(*num1*, [*num2*, ...*num255*])

The MIN function takes the following arguments:

- The first argument is a number, reference to cell with numeric value, or a cell range that contains numeric values.

- The arguments num2 to num255 are optional. They can take a number, reference to cell with numeric value, or a cell range that contains numeric values.

Example

In Figure 7-12, in cell C14, we have used the function =MIN(C2:C12). This will find the minimum number in the cell range C2 to C12. Since 23 is the minimum number, the function returns the value *23*.

MAXIFS Function

The MAXIFS function is used find the maximum value from a range based on one or more conditions.

Syntax

=MAXIFS (*max_range, range1, criteria1, [range2], [criteria2], ...*)

The MAXIFS function expects the following arguments:

- The first argument is the cell range from which to determine the maximum value.

- The second argument is the range to check for the criteria. You can use wildcards in the criteria. A question mark (?) is used to match any single character, while an asterisk (*) is used to match any number of characters.

Note   Criteria that includes text or logical or mathematical operators must be enclosed in double quotation marks (").

- The third argument is the criteria to check for.

- The MAXIFS function can take up to 126 range/criteria pairs. You have to ensure that each of the criteria ranges supplied is of the same size as the max_range.

Note   The MAXIFS function is available only in Microsoft 365 or Office 2019.

Example

Figure 7-13 shows an example of the MAXIFS and MINIFS functions. We will look into the MINIFS function shortly.

	A	B	C	D	E	F	G
1							
2	Name	Subject	Marks			Max	Min
3	Ashok	English	75		English	75	65
4	Rohit	English	65		Maths	89	70
5	Rashi	English	72				
6	Alisha	English	68				
7	Dilip	English	71				
8	Ashok	Maths	70				
9	Rohit	Maths	78				
10	Rashi	Maths	82				
11	Alisha	Maths	77				
12	Dilip	Maths	89				

Figure 7-13. *MAXIFS and MINIFS functions*

In Figure 7-13, we have data in cells A2 to C12.

In cell F3 we have used the function =MAXIFS(Table1[Marks],Table1 [Subject],E3). Here, we are asking for the maximum marks where the subject is English. This will return the value *75*.

In cell F4 we have used the function =MAXIFS(Table1[Marks],Table1 [Subject],E4). Here, we are asking for the maximum marks where the subject is Math. This will return the value *89*.

MINIFS Function

The MINIFS function is used find the minimum value from a range based on one or more conditions.

Syntax

=MINIFS (*min_range, range1, criteria1, [range2], [criteria2], ...*)

The MINIFS function expects the following arguments:

- The first argument is the cell range from which to determine the minimum value.

- The second argument is the range to check for the criteria. You can use wildcards in the criteria. A question mark (?) is used to match any single character, while an asterisk (*) is used to match any number of characters.

Note   Criteria that includes text or logical or mathematical operators must be enclosed in double quotation marks (").

- The third argument is the criteria to check for.

The MINIFS function can take up to 126 range/criteria pairs. You have to ensure that each of the criteria ranges supplied is of the same size as the min_range.

Note   The MINIFS function is available only in Microsoft 365 or Office 2019.

Example

In Figure 7-13, we have data in cells A2 to C12.

In cell G3 we have used the function =MINIFS(Table1[Marks],Table1[Subject],E3). Here, we are asking for the minimum marks where the subject is English. This will return the value *65*.

In cell G4 we have used the function =MINIFS(Table1[Marks],Table1[Subject],E4). Here, we are asking for the minimum marks where the subject is Math. This will return the value *70*.

Summary

In this chapter, we looked into the aggregate functions provided by Excel. As always, I suggest you try out the examples from this chapter using your own data and also using the different options for the arguments. This will give you more clarity regarding how the functions actually work.

In the next chapter, we will look into the logical functions available in Excel.

CHAPTER 8

Logical Functions

In this chapter, we will look at some of the logical functions provided by Excel. Logical functions evaluate a condition and return TRUE or FALSE depending on the result.

Let us look at some of the most commonly used logical functions of Excel.

IF Function

The IF function is used to evaluate a condition and return one value if the condition is true and another value if the condition is false.

Syntax

=IF(*condition, true value, false value*)

The IF condition takes three arguments, as follows:

- The first argument is the condition to be evaluated.

- The second argument is the value that is returned if the condition is true.

- The third argument is the value that is returned if the condition is false.

© Mandeep Mehta 2021
M. Mehta, *Microsoft Excel Functions Quick Reference*,
https://doi.org/10.1007/978-1-4842-6613-7_8

Note You can nest up to seven IF functions within either the TRUE value part or the FALSE value part. The condition should evaluate to a Boolean value of TRUE or FALSE, else the IF function will return an error.

Example

Figure 8-1 shows examples of the IF function.

◢	A	B	C
1	Name	Age	Adult/Child
2	Rohan	25	Adult
3	Richa	20	Adult
4	Ashok	15	Child
5	Tony	10	Child

Figure 8-1. *IF function*

In Figure 8-1, we have the names and ages of a few people. In column C we try to figure out if the person is an adult or a child. For this example, we treat anyone who is eighteen years or older as an adult and anyone under eighteen years old as a child.

In cell C2 we have used the formula =IF(B2>=18, "Adult", "Child"). Here, we are saying if the value in cell B2 is 18 or more then return the value *Adult*; else return the value *Child*. Copy the formula in cell C2 to cells C3, C4, and C5.

AND Function

The AND function is used to check if all the conditions given are true. The AND function is generally used with other Excel functions.

Syntax

=AND(*condition1, condition2, ... condition255*)

The AND function can take up to 255 arguments. The arguments to the AND function are the conditions that need to be evaluated. If all conditions are true, the AND function returns the Boolean value *TRUE*. If any of the conditions passed is false, the AND function returns the Boolean value *FALSE*.

Example

Figure 8-2 shows an example of the AND function.

	A	B
1		
2	Age	45
3		TRUE

***Figure 8-2.** AND function*

In cell B3 we have used the function =AND(B2>=1, B2<=100). Here, we check if the age given in cell B2 is between 1 and 100. The first condition checks if 45 is equal to or greater than 1. The second condition checks if 45 is less than or equal to 100. Since both the conditions are true, the AND function returns the value *TRUE*. If we change the value in B2 to a value more than 100, the AND function in cell C3 will return the value *FALSE*.

Figure 8-3 shows an example where the AND function is used with the IF function.

	A	B	C
1	Name	Age	Adult/Child
2	Rohan	25	Adult
3	Richa	20	Adult
4	Ashok	15	Teenager
5	Tony	10	Child

Figure 8-3. *IF with AND function*

In Figure 8-3, in cell C2, we have used the formula =IF(B2>18,"Adult",
IF(AND(B2>=0,B2<=12),"Child", "Teenager")). Here, the formula is
evaluated as follows:

- First, the value in cell B2 is checked to see if it is greater
  than 18. If it is greater than 18, the value *Adult* is
  returned.

- If the value in cell B2 is less than 18, then we check if
  the value in B2 is both greater than or equal to 0 and
  less than or equal to 12. If the value in B2 is between 0
  and 12 , the value *Child* is returned.

- If the previous two conditions fail, the value *Teenager* is
  returned.

OR Function

The OR function is used to check if any of the conditions given are true.
The OR function is generally used with other Excel functions.

Syntax

=OR(*condition1, condition2, ... condition255*)

The OR function can take up to 255 arguments. The arguments to the OR function are the conditions that need to be evaluated. If any of the conditions are true, the OR function returns the Boolean value *TRUE*. If all of the conditions passed are false, the OR function returns the Boolean value *FALSE*.

Example

Figure 8-4 shows an example of the OR function.

▲	A	B
1		
2	Fruit	Mango or Orange
3	Mango	TRUE
4	Orange	TRUE
5	Apple	FALSE
6	Banana	FALSE

Figure 8-4. *OR function*

In cell B3 we have used the function =OR(A3="Mango", A3="Orange"). Here, we are checking if the fruit name given in cell A3 is *Mango* or *Orange*. If the value is *Mango* or *Orange*, the OR function will return *TRUE*; else it will return *FALSE*. Copy the formula in cell B3 and paste it into the cells B4 to B6.

NOT Function

The NOT function converts the *TRUE* value to *FALSE* and the *FALSE* value to *TRUE*.

Syntax

=NOT(logical value)

The NOT function expects only one argument, as follows:

- An expression evaluating to a Boolean value of *TRUE* or *FALSE*. This can be a cell reference, a formula, or a function.

Example

Figure 8-5 shows an example of the NOT function.

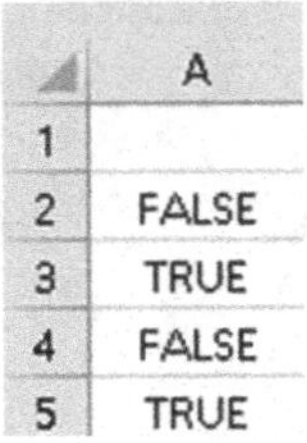

	A
1	
2	FALSE
3	TRUE
4	FALSE
5	TRUE

Figure 8-5. *NOT function*

The formula used is shown in Table 8-1.

Table 8-1. *Formula Used in Figure 8-5*

Cell Reference	Formula Used
A2	=NOT(TRUE)
A3	=NOT(FALSE)
A4	=NOT(10>5)
A5	=NOT(5>10)

XOR Function

The XOR function is also called the EXCLUSIVE OR function. When two logical statements are used, XOR will return

- *TRUE* if any of the conditions is *TRUE*, or

- *FALSE* if all conditions are *TRUE*.

When more than two logical statements are used in the XOR function, the return value will be

- *TRUE*, if the number of the conditions that evaluate to *TRUE* is an odd number; or

- *FALSE*, if the total number of conditions that evaluate to *TRUE* is an even number, or if all conditions are *FALSE*.

Syntax

=XOR(*condition1, condition2, ... condition255*)

The XOR function can take up to 255 arguments. The arguments to the XOR function are the conditions that need to be evaluated.

Example

Figure 8-6 shows an example of the XOR function.

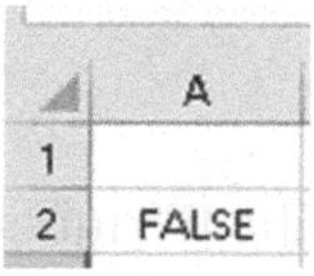

Figure 8-6. *XOR function*

In Figure 8-6, in cell A2, we have used the function =XOR(10>2, 2>5,1<3). The value returned is *FALSE*. In this case, since two conditions are *TRUE*, XOR returns the value *FALSE*. We have seen that if the number of conditions that evaluate to *TRUE* is an even number, XOR returns *FALSE*.

IFS Function

The IFS function is used to evaluate multiple conditions and returns a value that corresponds to the first *TRUE* condition. The IFS condition can be used to replace nested IF functions. Also, the IFS function is easy to read as compared to nested IF conditions. If none of the conditions evaluate to *TRUE*, the IFS function will return the #N/A error. Unlike the IF function, the IFS function does not have an ELSE part. But we can overcome this limitation, as we will see in the example section.

Note   The IFS function is available only in Microsoft 365 or Office 2019.

Syntax

=IFS(*condition1, value1, condition2, value2, ...*)

The IFS function can take up to 127 pairs of conditions to check and the value to return if the condition is *TRUE*.

Example

Figure 8-7 shows an example of the IFS function.

⬦	A	B
1		
2	Day number	
3	1	Monday

Figure 8-7. *IFS function*

In Figure 8-7, in cell A3, we have the weekday number. In cell B3, we have the function =IFS(A3=1, "Monday", A3=2, "Tuesday", A3=3, "Wednesday", A3=4, "Thursday", A3=5, "Friday", A3=6, "Saturday", A3=7, "Sunday"). As A3 contains the value 1, the value returned in B3 is *Monday*.

Let's say we change the formula in cell B3 to =IFS(A3=1, "Monday", A3=2, "Tuesday", A3=3, "Wednesday", A3=4, "Thursday", A3=5, "Friday", A3=6, "Saturday"). We also change the value in cell A3 to 7. The formula in cell B3 will evaluate to an #N/Λ error.

To overcome this, we can create a makeshift ELSE condition in the IFS function. Now, change the formula in cell B3 to =IFS(A3=1, "Monday", A3=2, "Tuesday", A3=3, "Wednesday", A3=4, "Thursday", A3=5, "Friday", A3=6, "Saturday", TRUE, "Sunday"). Here, we are checking if the value in cell A3 is from 1 to 6 and, if not, return the value *Sunday* instead of the #N/A error. So, any number other than 0 (besides the numbers 1 to 6, since these values are already handled) will evaluate to *TRUE*.

SWITCH Function

The SWITCH function is used to compare one value against a list of values and return a result corresponding to the first matching value. The SWITCH function can return an optional default value in case no match is found.

Note   The SWITCH function is available only in Microsoft 365 or Office 2019.

Syntax

=SWITCH(*expression, value1, result1, ...value126, result126,* [*default value*])

The SWITCH function takes the following arguments:

- The first argument is the expression to check for.

- The second argument is the value to be checked with the expression.

- The third argument is the result to be returned when value *1* matches the expression.

- The last argument is the value to be used in case no value matches the expression. This is like the default value.

You can have up to 126 value-result combinations in the SWITCH function.

Example

Figure 8-8 shows an example of the SWITCH function.

◢	A	B
1		
2	Day number	
3	7	Sunday

Figure 8-8. *SWITCH function*

In Figure 8-8, in cell B3, we have used the function =SWITCH(A3, 1, "Monday", 2, "Tuesday", 3, "Wednesday", 4, "Thursday", 5, "Friday", 6, "Saturday", 7, "Sunday"). Here, we are checking for the expression in A3 and, depending on the value, returning the corresponding result. The function in cell B3 could also be written as =SWITCH(A3, 1, "Monday", 2, "Tuesday", 3, "Wednesday", 4, "Thursday", 5, "Friday", 6, "Saturday", "Sunday").

Summary

In this chapter, we looked into the logical functions provided by Excel. As always, I suggest you try out the examples from this chapter using your own data and also using the different options for the arguments. This will give you more clarity regarding how the functions actually work.

In the next chapter, we will look into some of the commonly used math functions available in Excel.

CHAPTER 9

Math Functions

In this chapter, we will look at some of the math functions provided by Excel.

Note In the text functions in this chapter, the argument *number* can be

- a literal numeric value,
- an Excel function returning a numeric value,
- a cell reference where the cell contains a numeric value, or
- a named range referring to numeric values.

ABS Function

The ABS function returns the absolute value of a number without the sign. Negative numbers passed are converted to positive numbers, whereas positive numbers are unaffected.

Syntax

=ABS(*number*)

The ABS function takes only one argument, as follows:

© Mandeep Mehta 2021
M. Mehta, *Microsoft Excel Functions Quick Reference,*
https://doi.org/10.1007/978-1-4842-6613-7_9

- The number whose absolute value is to be returned. This argument can be a cell reference containing a numeric value, a function returning a numeric value, or a literal numeric number.

Example

Table 9-1 shows examples of the ABS function.

Table 9-1. *ABS Function*

Function Used	Result	Comments
=ABS(-29)	29	The value is returned without the minus '-' sign.
=ABS(29)	29	Since we have passed a positive number to the ABS function, the number is returned as it is.

INT Function

The INT function is used to return the integer part of a decimal number, rounded down to the nearest integer.

SYNTAX

=INT(*number*)

The INT function expects only one argument, as follows:

- A decimal number that needs to be rounded down to the nearest integer. A negative number will become more negative.

Example

Table 9-2 shows examples of the INT function.

Table 9-2. *INT Function*

Function Used	Result	Comments
=INT(14.567)	14	This will return the value *14*.
=INT(-14.567)	-15	This will return the value integer part *-15*. So, you see, a negative number becomes more negative.

TRUNC Function

The TRUNC function is used to truncate a decimal number to a specified number of digits.

Syntax

=TRUNC(*number, [number of digits]*)

The TRUNC function takes the following arguments:

- The first argument is the decimal number.

- The second argument is the number of digits to keep in the final output. This argument is optional. If this argument has a value of *0* or is omitted, the decimal part is removed.

Example

Table 9-3 shows examples of the TRUNC function.

153

Table 9-3. *TRUNC Function Examples*

Function Used	Return Value	Description
=TRUNC(14.567,3)	14.567	Truncates the value 14.567 to 3 decimal places
=TRUNC(14.567,2)	14.56	Truncates the value 14.567 to 2 decimal places
=TRUNC(14.567,1)	14.5	Truncates the value 14.567 to 1 decimal place
=TRUNC(14.567,0)	14	Returns the integer part of the decimal number in the value 14.567
=TRUNC(14.567)	14	Returns the integer part of the decimal number in the value 14.567

ROUND Function

The ROUND function is used to round a number to a specific number of digits.

Syntax

=ROUND(*number*, [*number of digits*])

The ROUND function takes the following arguments:

- The first argument is the number to be rounded.

- The second argument is the number of digits to which the number is to be rounded.

Example

Table 9-4 shows examples of the ROUND function.

Table 9-4. *ROUND Function Examples*

Function Used	Return Value	Description
=ROUND(1265.867812,3)	1265.868	Returns the number rounded to 3 decimal places
=ROUND(1265.867812,2)	1265.87	Returns the number rounded to 2 decimal places
=ROUND(1265.867812,1)	1265.9	Returns the number rounded to 1 decimal place
=ROUND(1265.867812,0)	1266	Returns the number rounded to the nearest integer
=ROUND(1265.867812,-1)	1270	Returns the number rounded to the nearest multiple of 10
=ROUND(1265.867812,-2)	1300	Returns the number rounded to the nearest multiple of 100
=ROUND(1265.867812,-3)	1000	Returns the number rounded to the nearest multiple of 1000

CEILING Function

The CEILING function is used to round a number up to the nearest specified multiple.

Syntax

=CEILING(*number, significance*)

The CEILING function takes two arguments, as follows:

- The first argument is the number to be rounded up.

- The second argument is the multiple to which the number is to be rounded up.

155

Example

Table 9-5 shows examples of CEILING function.

Table 9-5. *CEILING Function Examples*

Function Used	Return Value	Description
=CEILING(1265.5, 3)	1266	Rounds up a number to the multiple of 3
=CEILING(1265.5, 10)	1270	Rounds up a number to the multiple of 10
=CEILING(-1265.5, -1)	-1266	Rounds up a negative number to the multiple of -1
=CEILING(-1265.5, -5)	-1270	Rounds up a negative number to the multiple of -5
=CEILING(-1265.5, -20)	-1280	Rounds up a negative number to the multiple of -20
=CEILING(1265.387, 0.5)	1265.5	Rounds up the number to the nearest multiple of 0.5
=CEILING(1265.387, 0.1)	1265.4	Rounds up the number to the nearest multiple of 0.1

FLOOR Function

The FLOOR function is used to round a number down to the nearest specified multiple.

Syntax

=FLOOR(*number, significance*)

The FLOOR function takes two arguments, as follows:

- The first argument is the number to round down.

- The second argument is the multiple to which the number is to be rounded down.

Example

Table 9-6 shows examples of the FLOOR function.

Table 9-6. *FLOOR Function Examples*

Function Used	Return Value	Description
=FLOOR(1265.5, 3)	1263	Rounds down a number to the multiple of 3
=FLOOR(1265.5, 10)	1260	Rounds down a number to the multiple of 10
=FLOOR(-1265.5, -1)	-1265	Rounds down a negative number to the multiple of -1
=FLOOR(-1265.5, -5)	-1265	Rounds down a negative number to the multiple of -5
=FLOOR(-1265.5, -20)	-1260	Rounds down a negative number to the multiple of -20
=FLOOR(1265.387, 0.75)	1265.25	Rounds down the number to the nearest multiple of 0.75
=FLOOR(1265.387, 0.3)	1265.1	Rounds down the number to the nearest multiple of 0.3

RAND Function

The RAND function is used to generate a number greater than or equal to 0 and less than 1. The RAND function returns a new random number every time your spreadsheet opens or calculates.

Syntax

=RAND()

The RAND function does not take any argument.

Example

Table 9-7 shows examples of the RAND function.

Table 9-7. *RAND Function Examples*

Function Used	Return Value
=RAND()	0.095883659
=RAND()	0.774144656
=RAND()	0.694113397
=RAND()	0.058422166
=RAND()	0.550188071

Note   The values returned by RAND() function on your system will be different.

RANDBETWEEN Function

The RANDBETWEEN function is used to generate random numbers between two specified numbers.

Syntax

=RANDBETWEEN(*start number, end number*)

The RANDBETWEEN function takes two arguments, as follows:

- The first argument is the lower of the two numbers.
- The second argument is the higher of the two numbers.

Example

Table 9-8 shows examples of the RANDBETWEEN function. The examples in Table 9-8 return a random number between 1 and 100.

Table 9-8. *RANDBETWEEN Function Examples*

Function Used	Return Value
= RANDBETWEEN (1,100)	82
= RANDBETWEEN (1,100)	5
= RANDBETWEEN (1,100)	18
= RANDBETWEEN (1,100)	51
= RANDBETWEEN (1,100)	87

Note   The values returned by the RANDBETWEEN() function on your system will be different.

Summary

In this chapter, we looked into some of the math functions provided by Excel. As always, I suggest you try out the examples from this chapter using your own data and also using the different options for the arguments. This will give you more clarity regarding how the functions actually work.

In the next chapter, we will look into some of the most commonly used information functions available in Excel.

CHAPTER 10

Information Functions

In this chapter, we will look into some of the information functions provided by Excel. These functions give information about the contents of a cell, formula, sheet, worksheet, or operating environment.

Let us now look into the information functions.

CELL Function

The CELL function is used to return information about a cell, or the first cell if it is a range.

Syntax

=CELL(*info_type*, [*reference*])

The CELL function takes two arguments, as follows:

- The first argument is the type of information to return about the reference. Table 10-1 shows the values that this argument can take. The value for this argument should be enclosed in double quotes ("").

- The second argument is the reference from which to extract information. This argument is optional. If this argument is omitted, the information about the current cell is returned.

© Mandeep Mehta 2021
M. Mehta, *Microsoft Excel Functions Quick Reference*,
https://doi.org/10.1007/978-1-4842-6613-7_10

Table 10-1. *Arguments for the Info Type Argument*

Value	Return Value
address	Returns the address of the cell. If the cell refers to a range, it will return the address of the first cell in the range.
col	Returns the column number of the cell.
color	Returns *1* if the cell is color formatted for negative values; else it returns *0.*
contents	Returns the contents of the cell. If the cell contains a formula, the value of the formula is returned.
filename	Returns the filename of the file that contains the reference.
format	Returns a code that corresponds to the number format of the cell reference. Table 10-2 shows the formats.
parentheses	Returns *1* if the cell is formatted with parentheses; else it returns *0.*
prefix	• Returns a single quote (') if the cell is left-aligned. • Returns a double quote (") if the cell is right-aligned. • Returns a caret (^) if the cell is center-aligned. • Returns a backslash (\) if the cell is fill-aligned. • Returns an empty text value for all others.
protect	Returns *1* if the cell is locked. Returns *0* if the cell is not locked.
row	Returns the row number of the cell.
type	Returns the value *b* if the cell is empty. Returns the value *l* if the cell contains a text constant. Returns the value *v* for all others.
width	Returns the column width of the cell, rounded to the nearest integer.

Table 10-2. *Format Codes Used in the CELL Function*

Format of the Cell	Returned Value
General	G
0	F0
0	F2
#,##0	,0
#,##0.00	,2
Currency with no decimal places $#,##0 or $#,##0_);($#,##0)	C0
Currency with 2 decimal places $#,##0.00 or $#,##0.00_);($#,##0.00)	C2
Percentage with no decimal places 0%	P0
Percentage with 2 decimal places 0.00%	P2
Scientific notation 0.00E+00	S2
Fraction # ?/? or # ??/??	G
m/d/yy or m/d/yy h:mm or mm/dd/yy	D4
d-mmm-yy or dd-mmm-yy	D1
d-mmm or dd-mmm	D2
mmm-yy	D3
mm/dd	D5
h:mm AM/PM	D7
h:mm:ss AM/PM	D6
h:mm	D9
h:mm:ss	D8

163

Example

Table 10-3 shows examples of the CELL function used in Figure 10-1.

Table 10-3. *Examples of the CELL Function Used in Figure 10-1*

Cell Reference	Formula Used	Return Value	Comments
B4	=CELL("address",A2)	$A$2	Returns the cell address
B5	=CELL("col",A2)	1	Return column number *1*
B6	=CELL("color",A2)	0	Returns *0*, as the cell is not formatted with color
B7	=CELL("contents",A2)	Cell Function	Returns the cell value
B8	=CELL("format",A2)	G	Returns *G* to indicate General format
B9	=CELL("parentheses",A2)	0	Returns *0* as the cell is not formatted with parentheses
B10	=CELL("prefix",A2)	^	Returns ^ as the text is centered
B11	=CELL("protect",A2)	1	Returns *1* as the cell is locked (This is the default state.)
B12	=CELL("row",A2)	2	Returns rows number *2*
B13	=CELL("type",A2)	l	Returns *l* as the cell contains text
B14	=CELL("width",A2)	22	Returns the width of the column

	A	B
1		
2	Cell Function	
3		
4		$A$2
5		1
6		0
7		Cell Function
8		G
9		0
10		^
11		1
12		2
13		l
14		17

Figure 10-1. CELL function

INFO Function

The INFO function returns information about the current operating environment.

Syntax

=INFO(*text*)

The INFO function takes only one argument, as follows:

- The first argument is used to specify what type of information is required. Table 10-4 shows the values that can be given for this argument. The value passed for this argument can only be one of the values from Table 10-4.

165

Table 10-4. *Arguments for the INFO Function*

Value Used	Information Returned
"directory"	Returns the path of the current directory
"numfile"	Returns the number of active worksheets in all currently open Excel workbooks
"origin"	Returns the absolute cell reference of the top and leftmost cell visible in the window
"osversion"	Returns the current operating system version
"recalc"	Returns the current recalculation mode (whether "Automatic" or "Manual")
"release"	Returns the current version of Microsoft Excel
"system"	Returns the current operating environment ("mac" for Macintosh, "pcdos" for Windows)

Example

Table 10-5 shows examples of the INFO function.

Table 10-5. *INFO Function*

Function Used	Return Value
=INFO("NUMFILE")	4
=INFO("ORIGIN")	$A:$A$1
=INFO("OSVERSION")	Windows (32-bit) NT 10.00
=INFO("RECALC")	Automatic
=INFO("RELEASE")	16.0
=INFO("SYSTEM")	pcdos

Note   The return values on your system could be different.

ISBLANK Function

The ISBLANK function is used to check if a cell is blank.

Syntax

=ISBLANK(*reference*)

The ISBLANK function takes only one argument, as follows:

- The cell reference to check if it is blank

The function will return *TRUE* if the cell is blank; else it returns *FALSE*.

Example

Table 10-6 shows examples of the ISBLANK function.

Table 10-6. ISBLANK Function

Cell Reference	Cell Contents	Function Used	Return Value
A1	Cell A1 is empty	=ISBLANK(A1)	*TRUE*, because cell A1 is empty
A2	This cell has content	=ISBLANK(A2)	*FALSE*, because cell A2 is not empty

ISERROR Function

The ISERROR function is used to check if a cell or formula contains an error.

Syntax

=ISERROR(*value*)

The ISERROR function takes only one argument, as follows:

- The value to check if the cell or formula contains an error. The value can be a cell reference, a literal value, or a function that returns a value.

The function will return *TRUE* if the cell has an error; else it returns *FALSE*.

Example

Table 10-7 shows examples of the ISERROR function.

Table 10-7. *ISERROR Function*

Cell Reference	Cell Contents	Function Used	Return Value
A1	Cell A1 is empty	=ISERROR(A1)	*FALSE*, because cell A1 is empty
A2	=10/0	=ISERROR(A2)	*TRUE*, because cell A2 results in an error #DIV/0!

ISEVEN Function

The ISEVEN function checks if the specified value is an even number.

Syntax

=ISEVEN(*value*)

The ISEVEN function takes only one argument, as follows:

- The value to check if the value is an even number. The value can be a literal numeric value or a cell reference containing a numeric value or a formula that returns a numeric value.

The function will return *TRUE* if the value is an even number; else it returns *FALSE*.

Example

Table 10-8 shows examples of the ISEVEN function.

Table 10-8. *ISEVEN Function*

Cell Reference	Cell Contents	Function Used	Return Value
A1	5	=ISEVEN(A1)	*FALSE*, as value in cell A1 is an odd number
A2	10	=ISEVEN(A2)	*TRUE*, as value in cell A2 is an even number

169

ISODD Function

The ISODD function checks if the specified value is an odd number.

Syntax

=ISODD(*value*)

The ISODD function takes only one argument, as follows:

- The value to check if the value is odd. The value can be a literal numeric value or a cell reference containing a numeric value or a formula that returns a numeric value.

The function will return *TRUE* if the value is an odd number; else it returns *FALSE*.

Example

Table 10-9 shows examples of the ISODD function.

Table 10-9. *ISODD Function*

Cell Reference	Cell Contents	Function Used	Return Value
A1	5	=ISODD(A1)	*TRUE*, as value in cell A1 is an odd number
A2	10	=ISODD(A2)	*FALSE*, as value in cell A2 is an even number

ISFORMULA Function

The ISFORMULA function checks if the cell reference is a formula.

Syntax

`=ISFORMULA(cell reference)`

The ISFORMULA function takes only one argument, as follows:

- The cell reference to check if the cell contains a formula

The function will return *TRUE* if the cell contains a formula; else it returns *FALSE*.

Example

Table 10-10 shows examples of the ISFORMULA function.

Table 10-10. ISFORMULA Function

Cell Reference	Cell A1 Is Empty	Function Used	Return Value
A1	=10*2	=ISFORMULA(A1)	*TRUE*, as cell A1 contains a formula
A2	10	=ISFORMULA(A2)	*FALSE*, as cell A2 contains a value

ISLOGICAL Function

The ISLOGICAL function checks if the specified value is either TRUE or FALSE.

Syntax

`=ISLOGICAL(value)`

The ISLOGICAL function takes only one argument, as follows:

- The value to check if the value is a Boolean or not. The value can be a literal Boolean value or a cell reference containing a Boolean value or formula that returns a Boolean value.

The function will return *TRUE* if the value is a Boolean value; else it returns *FALSE*.

Example

Table 10-11 shows examples of the ISLOGICAL function.

Table 10-11. *ISLOGICAL Function*

Cell Reference	Value in Cell Reference	Function Used	Return Value
A1	=10=2	=ISLOGICAL(A1)	*TRUE*, as the formula in cell A1 evaluates to TRUE
A2	10	=ISLOGICAL(A2)	*FALSE*, as cell A2 contains a numeric value

ISNA Function

The ISNA function checks if the specified value is the error value #N/A.

Syntax

`=ISNA(value)`

The ISNA function takes only one argument, as follows:

- The value to check if the value is #N/A or not. The value can be a cell reference containing an #N/A value or a formula that returns a value.

The function will return *TRUE* if the value is an #N/A; else it returns *FALSE*.

Example

Table 10-12 shows examples of the ISNA function.

Table 10-12. ISNA Function

Cell Reference	Value in Cell Reference	Function Used	Return Value
A1	=NA()	=ISNA(A1)	*TRUE*, as cell A1 contains a formula that returns *#N/A*
A2	10	=ISNA(A2)	FALSE, as cell A2 contains a numeric value

ISNONTEXT Function

The ISNONTEXT function is used to check if the value contains a text or not.

Syntax

=ISNONTEXT(*value*)

The ISNONTEXT function takes only one argument, as follows:

- The value to check whether it contains text. The value can be a cell reference, a literal value, or a function that returns a value.

If the value is not text, the function returns *TRUE*; else it returns *FALSE*.

Example

Table 10-13 shows examples of the ISNONTEXT function.

Table 10-13. *ISNONTEXT Function*

Function Used	Result
=ISNONTEXT("This is a text")	*FALSE*, as the value passed is text
=ISNONTEXT(123)	TRUE, as the value passed is a number
=ISNONTEXT(TODAY())	*TRUE*, as the value passed is a date. TODAY() function returns the current system date

ISNUMBER Function

The ISNUMBER function is used to check if the value contains a number.

Syntax

=ISNUMBER(*value*)

The ISNUMBER function takes only one argument, as follows:

- The value to check whether it contains a number. The value can be a cell reference, a literal value, or a function that returns a value.

If the value is a number, the function returns a *TRUE*; else it returns a *FALSE*.

Example

Table 10-14 shows examples of the ISNUMBER function.

Table 10-14. ISNUMBER Function

Function Used	Result
=ISNUMBER(1234)	*TRUE*, as the value passed is a number
=ISNUMBER("This is a text")	*FALSE*, as the value passed is a text

ISREF Function

The ISREF function is used to check if the value passed is a reference.

Syntax

=ISREF(*value*)

The ISREF function takes only one argument, as follows:

- The value to check whether it contains a cell reference. The value can be a cell reference, a literal value, or a function.

If the value is a cell reference, the function returns a *TRUE*; else it returns a *FALSE*.

Example

Table 10-15 shows examples of the ISREF function.

Table 10-15. *ISREF Function*

Function Used	Result
=ISREF(A1)	*TRUE*, as the value passed is a cell reference
=ISREF("This is a text")	*FALSE*, as the value passed is a text
=ISREF(TODAY())	*FALSE*

ISTEXT Function

The ISTEXT function is used to check if the value contains text.

Syntax

=ISTEXT(*value*)

The ISTEXT function takes only one argument, as follows:

- The value to check whether it contains text. The value can be a cell reference, a literal value, or a function that returns a value.

If the value is text, the function returns a *TRUE*; else it returns a *FALSE*.

Example

Table 10-16 shows examples of the ISTEXT function.

Table 10-16. *ISTEXT Function*

Function Used	Result
=ISTEXT(1234)	*FALSE*, as the value passed is a number
=ISTEXT("This is a text")	*TRUE*, as the value passed is text

N Function

The N function converts the value passed to a number.

Syntax

=N(*value*). The N function takes only one argument, as follows:

- The value to convert to a number. The value can be a cell reference, a literal value, or a function that returns a value.

Table 10-17 shows the return values for the N function.

Table 10-17. *N Function Return Values*

Value Passed to the N Function	Return Value
Number	A number
Date	Returns the date as a serial number
TRUE	1
FALSE	0
If the value is an error	Error
All other values	0

Example

Table 10-18 shows examples of the N function.

Table 10-18. *N Function*

Function Used	Result
=N(1234)	1234
=N("This is a text")	0
=N(TRUE)	1
=N(FALSE)	0

NA Function

The NA function is used to generate the #N/A error to indicate a value is not available. This is generally used to mark empty cells. By using #N/A for cells that are missing data, you avoid the problem of unintentionally including empty cells in your calculations. So, when a formula refers to cells containing #N/A, the formula will also return the error value #N/A. The NA function is also useful when the data is used to plot charts, as charts do not plot #N/A errors, but they do plot zeros.

Syntax

=NA()

The NA function takes no argument. It returns the value *#N/A*.

Example

Table 10-19 shows an example of the NA function.

Table 10-19. *NA Function*

Function Used	Result
=NA()	#N/A
=IF(B4="", NA(), A4 * B4)	If cell B4 is empty, #N/A is returned; else the value in A4 is multiplied by the value in B4

SHEET Function

The SHEET function is used to return the sheet number of the referenced sheet.

Syntax

=SHEET([*value*])

The SHEET function can take one argument, as follows:

- The name of the sheet or the cell reference of the sheet whose sheet number you want. If this argument is omitted, the current sheet number is returned.

Example

Figure 10-2 shows examples of the SHEET function.

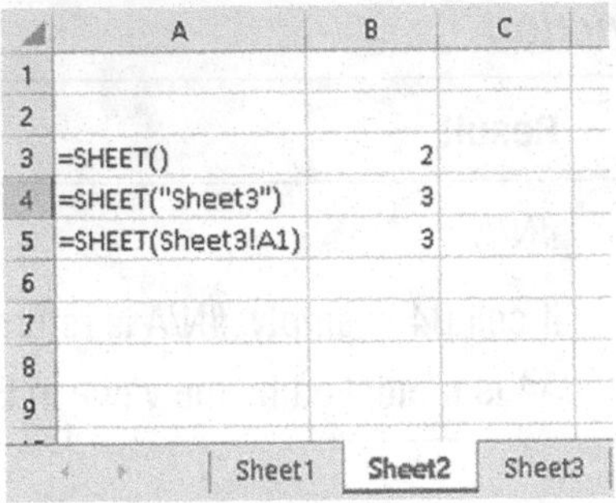

Figure 10-2. *SHEET function*

Table 10-20 shows the examples of the SHEET function shown in Figure 10-2.

Table 10-20. *SHEET Function*

Function Used	Result
=SHEET()	2. As you can see in Figure 10-2, the function was used in cell B3 in Sheet2.
=SHEET("Sheet3")	3, as Sheet3 is the third sheet in the sequence, as can be seen in Figure 10-2.
=SHEET(Sheet3!A1)	3. Here, we are referring to cell A1 in Sheet3, and Sheet3 is the third sheet in the sequence, as can be seen in Figure 10-2.

SHEETS Function

The SHEETS functions returns the number of sheets in the reference.

Syntax

=SHEETS([reference])

The SHEETS function takes an optional argument, as follows:

- The reference for which you want to know the number of sheets contained within. This argument is optional. If it is omitted, it returns the number of sheets in the current Excel workbook.

Example

Figure 10-3 shows examples of the SHEETS function.

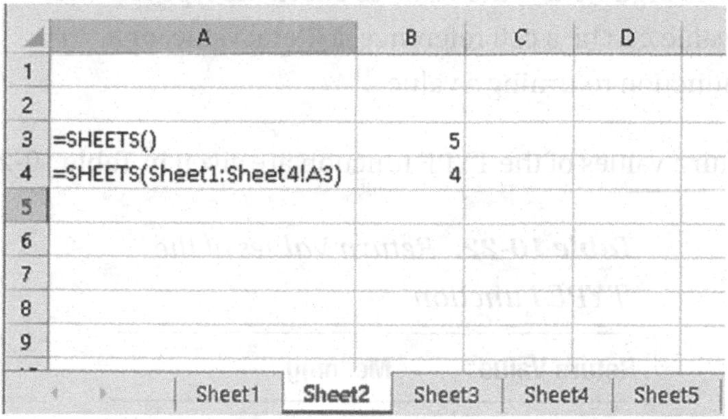

Figure 10-3. *SHEETS function*

Table 10-21 shows examples of the SHEETS function shown in Figure 10-3.

Table 10-21. *SHEETS Function*

Function Used	Result
=SHEETS()	5. As you can see in Figure 10-3, there are five sheets.
=SHEETS(Sheet1:Sheet4!A3)	4. Here we are referring to Sheet1 to Sheet 4.

TYPE Function

The TYPE function returns a numeric code depending on the type of the value in a cell.

Syntax

=TYPE(value)

The TYPE function takes only one argument, as follows:

- The argument is the value to check the type for. The value can be a cell reference, a literal value, or a function returning a value.

The return values of the TYPE function are given in Table 10-22.

Table 10-22. *Return Values of the TYPE Function*

Return Value	Meaning
1	Number value
2	Text value
4	Logical value
16	Error value
64	Array value

Example

Table 10-23 shows examples of the TYPE function.

Table 10-23. *TYPE Function*

Function Used	Return Value
=TYPE("abcd")	*2*, as the value passed is a text
=TYPE(123)	*1*, as the value passed is a number
=TYPE(NA())	*16*, as the value passed is an error value

Summary

In this chapter, we looked at some of the information functions provided by Excel. As always, I suggest you try out the examples from this chapter using your own data and also using the different options for the arguments. This will give you more clarity regarding how the functions actually work.

In the next chapter, we will look into commonly used financial functions in Excel.

CHAPTER 11

Finance Functions

In this chapter, we will look into some of the most commonly used finance functions provided by Excel for use in financial calculations. So, let us began.

FV Function

The FV function returns the future value of an investment that has periodic constant payments and a constant interest rate.

Syntax

=FV(*rate, period, payment,* [*present value*], [*type*])

The FV function takes the following arguments:

- The first argument is the interest rate for the period. Here, it is assumed that payment is made once per year. If the payment period is different, divide the rate accordingly. So,

  - if payment is monthly, divide the rate by 12; or

  - if payment is quarterly, divide the rate by 4.

© Mandeep Mehta 2021
M. Mehta, *Microsoft Excel Functions Quick Reference*,
https://doi.org/10.1007/978-1-4842-6613-7_11

- The second argument is the total number of payment periods. Here again, if the payment period is different, the number of payment periods has to be entered accordingly. So,

  - if payment is monthly, the number of periods will be 12; or

  - if payment is quarterly, the number of periods will be 4.

- The third argument is the payment made each period. If this argument is omitted, the present value (which is the fourth argument) must be given.

- The fourth argument is optional. The fourth argument specifies the present value. If this argument is omitted, it is considered to be zero.

- The fifth argument is the type. This argument is optional. This argument specifies if the payment is made at the beginning or the end of the period. It can have one the following values:

  - 0 – Indicates payment is made at the end of the period. The value *0* is used if this argument is omitted.

  - 1 – Indicates payment is made at the beginning of the period.

Example

Figure 11-1 shows an example of the FV function.

	A	B
1		
2	Rate	10%
3	No. of periods	5
4	Present vaue	$ 10,000.00
5		
6	Future Value	$ 16,105.10

Figure 11-1. *FV function*

In Figure 11-1, we are trying to get the future value of $10,000 invested at 10 percent yearly interest for a period of five years. The formula used in cell B6 is =FV(B2,B3,,-B4). The value returned is *$16,105.1*. What this indicates is that for an amount of $10,000 invested for five years at 10 percent interest compounded annually, the maturity amount will be $16,105.1.

Let us look at another example. Enter the following formula in a blank cell: =FV(10%/12,60,-1000). Here, we are trying to find out the future value of an investment of $1,000 per month for a period of five years. The interest is 10 percent per year, and each payment is made at the start of the month. The return value is $77,437.07.

In this example:

- Since the payments are made monthly, the annual interest rate of 10 percent has been converted into a monthly rate (=10%/12), and the five-year period has been input as a number of months (60).

- Also, since the monthly payments are paid out, we have used -1000 as input to the function.

PV Function

The PV function returns the present value of an investment based on a series of future payments.

Syntax

=PV(*rate, period, payment, [future value], [type]*)

The PV function takes the following arguments:

- The first argument is the interest rate for the period. Here, it is assumed that payment is made once per year. If the payment period is different, divide the rate accordingly. So,

  - if payment is monthly, divide the rate by 12; or

  - if payment is quarterly, divide the rate by 4.

- The second argument is the total number of payment periods. Here again, if the payment period is different, the number of payment periods has to be entered accordingly. So,

  - if payment is monthly, the number of periods will be 12; or

  - if payment is quarterly, the number of periods will be 4.

- The third argument is the payment made each period. If this argument is omitted, the future value (which is the fourth argument) must be given.

- The fourth argument is optional. The fourth argument specifies the future value. If this argument is omitted it is considered to be zero.

- The fifth argument is the type. This argument is optional. This argument specifies if the payment is made at the beginning or the end of the period. It can have one of the following values:

- 0 – Indicates payment is made at the end of the period. The value *0* is used if this argument is omitted.

- 1 – Indicates payment is made at the beginning of the period.

Example

Figure 11-2 shows an example of the PV function.

	A	B
1		
2	Rate	10%
3	No. of periods	5
4	Present vaue	$ 16,105.10
5		
6	Future Value	$ 10,000.00

Figure 11-2. *PV function*

In Figure 11-2, we are trying to get the present value of $16,105.1 invested at 10 percent yearly interest for a period of five years. The formula used in cell B6 is =PV(B2,B3,,-B4). The value returned is *$10,000*.

Let us look at another example. Enter the following formula in a blank cell: =PV(10%/12,60,,-5000). Here, we are trying to find out the present value of an investment that has a total value $5,000 after making monthly payments for five years. The interest is 10 percent per year, and each payment is made at the start of the quarter. The return value is *$3,038.94*.

In this example:

- Since the payments are made monthly, the annual interest rate of 10 percent has been converted into a monthly rate (=10%/12), and the five-year period has been input as a number of months (60).

189

- Also, since the monthly payments are paid out, we have used -5000 as input to the function.

PMT Function

The PMT function is used to calculate the periodic payment value. This is generally used to calculate the EMI of a loan.

Syntax

=PMT(*rate, period, present value, [future value], [type]*)

The PMT function takes the following arguments:

- The first argument is the interest rate for the period.

- The second argument is the number of periods over which the payment/investment is to be made.

- The third argument is the present value of the loan or investment.

- The fourth argument is optional. It specifies the future value of the loan or investment at the end of all payments. If this argument is omitted, it is considered to be zero.

- The fifth argument is the type. This argument is optional. This argument specifies if the payment is made at the beginning or the end of the period. It can have one the following values:

  - 0 – Indicates payment is made at the end of the period. The value *0* is used if this argument is omitted.

  - 1 – Indicates payment is made at the beginning of the period.

Example

For this example, the PMT function is used to calculate the monthly payments on a loan of $500,000 that is to be paid off in full after five years. Interest is charged at a rate of 10 percent per year, and the payment to the loan is to be made at the end of each month. Enter the following formula in a blank cell: =PMT(10%/12, 60, 500000).

The value returned is *$-10,623.52*. Here are some things to remember about this example:

- As the payments are made monthly, the annual interest rate of 10 percent is divided by 12 to convert it into the monthly rate, and the period of five years is converted in months (60).

- The future value and type arguments are omitted as the future value is zero, and the payment is to be made at the end of the month.

- The value returned from the function is negative, as this represents an outgoing payment for repayment of the loan taken.

IPMT Function

The IPMT function returns the interest payment for a specific period of a loan or investment where the payments and interest rates are constant.

Syntax

=IPMT(*rate, period, number of periods, present value, [future value], [type]*)

The IPMT function expects the following arguments:

- The first argument is interest rate for the period.

- The second argument is the period for which you want to find the interest. This value should be between 1 and the total number of periods.

- The third argument is the total number of periods.

- The fourth argument is the present value of the loan or investment.

- The fifth argument is optional. It is the future value at the end of the number of periods specified in the third argument. If this argument is omitted, future value is taken as zero.

- The sixth argument is the type. This argument is optional. This argument specifies if the payment is made at the beginning or the end of the period. It can have one the following values:

  - 0 – Indicates payment is made at the end of the period. The value *0* is used if this argument is omitted.

  - 1 – Indicates payment is made at the beginning of the period.

Example

Figure 11-3 shows an example of the IPMT function.

	A	B
1	Loan amount	$ 50,000
2	Interest rate	10%
3	Number of periods	12
4	1	$ -416.67
5	2	$ -383.51
6	3	$ -350.07
7	4	$ -316.36
8	5	$ -282.36
9	6	$ -248.08
10	7	$ -213.52
11	8	$ -178.67
12	9	$ -143.52
13	10	$ -108.09
14	11	$ -72.36
15	12	$ -36.33

Figure 11-3. *IPMT function*

In Figure 11-3, we have a loan amount of $50,000 to be paid back in twelve monthly installments. The interest rate is 10 percent. In cell B4 we have used the formula =IPMT($B$2/12,A4,$B$3,$B$1). This will return the value *$416.67*. This is the interest part of the loan installment for the first month. Copy the formula in cell B4 to cells B5 to B15. These will return the interest parts of the loan installments for the respective months. As you can see, the interest part keeps reducing as we move toward the end of the payment period.

PPMT Function

The PPMT functions returns the principal payment for a specific period of a loan or investment where the payments and interest rates are constant.

Syntax

=PPMT(rate, period, number of periods, present value, [future value], [type])

The PPMT function takes the following arguments:

- The first argument is the interest rate for the period.

- The second argument is the period for which you want to find the principal paid. This value should be between 1 and the total number of periods.

- The third argument is the total number of periods.

- The fourth argument is the present value of the loan or investment.

- The fifth argument is optional. It is the future value at the end of the number of periods specified in the third argument. If this argument is omitted, future value is taken as zero.

- The sixth argument is the type. This argument is optional. This argument specifies if the payment is made at the beginning or the end of the period. It can have one the following values:

  - 0 – Indicates payment is made at the end of the period. The value *0* is used if this argument is omitted.

  - 1 – Indicates payment is made at the beginning of the period.

Example

Figure 11-4 shows an example of the PPMT function.

◢	A	B
1	Loan amount	$ 50,000
2	Interest rate	10%
3	Number of periods	12
4	1	$ -3,979.13
5	2	$ -4,012.29
6	3	$ -4,045.72
7	4	$ -4,079.44
8	5	$ -4,113.43
9	6	$ -4,147.71
10	7	$ -4,182.28
11	8	$ -4,217.13
12	9	$ -4,252.27
13	10	$ -4,287.71
14	11	$ -4,323.44
15	12	$ -4,359.47

Figure 11-4. *PPMT function*

In Figure 11-4, we have a loan amount of $50,000 to be paid back in twelve monthly installments. The interest rate is 10 percent. In cell B4 we have used the formula =PPMT($B$2/12,A4,$B$3,$B$1). This will return the value *$3,979.13*. This is the principal part of the loan installment for the first month. Copy the formula in cell B4 to cells B5 to B15. These will return the principal parts of the loan installments for the respective months. As you can see, the principal part keeps increasing as we move toward the end of the payment period.

RATE Function

The RATE function is used to calculate the interest rate that would be required

- to pay off a loan, or

- to reach a target amount of investment.

Syntax

=RATE(*number of periods, payment amount per period, present value, [future value], [type], [guess]*)

The RATE function takes the following arguments:

- The first argument is the number of periods over which the loan/investment is to be paid off.

- The second argument is the fixed amount to be paid for each period.

- The third argument is the present value of the loan/ investment.

- The fourth argument is the future value; this argument is optional. If omitted it is considered as zero.

- The fifth argument is the type. This argument is optional. This argument specifies if the payment is made at the beginning or the end of the period. It can have one the following values:

  - 0 – Indicates payment is made at the end of the period. The value *0* is used if this argument is omitted.

  - 1 – Indicates payment is made at the beginning of the period.

- The sixth argument is the estimate of the interest rate. This argument is optional. If omitted, it is assumed to be 10 percent.

Example

In this example, we are trying to calculate the interest rate to pay off a loan amount of $80,000 over a period of four years with a fixed monthly payment of $2,000. Enter the following formula in a blank cell: =RATE(4*12,-2000,80000). This will return *0.77* percent. Since this is the monthly rate, we need to convert it into an annual rate by multiplying it by twelve. So, change the formula you just entered to make it look like the following formula: =RATE(4*12,-2000,80000) *12. This will return *9.24* percent, which is the annual rate.

NPER Function

The NPER function is used to calculate the number of periods required to pay off a loan wherein the periodic payment amount and interest rate are constant.

Syntax

=NPER(*interest rate, periodic payment amount, present value, [future value], [type]*)

The NPER function takes the following arguments:

- The first argument is the interest rate.

- The second argument is the periodic payment amount.

- The third argument is the present value of the loan.

- The fourth argument specifies the future value of the loan. This argument is optional. If omitted, this value is taken as zero.

- The fifth argument is the type. This argument is optional. This argument specifies if the payment is made at the beginning or the end of the period. It can have one the following values:

    - 0 – Indicates payment is made at the end of the period. The value *0* is used if this argument is omitted.

    - 1 – Indicates payment is made at the beginning of the period.

Example

In this example, we try to calculate the number of periods required to pay off a loan of $500,000 at the rate of $120,000 per year. The interest rate charged is 10 percent. The payment is made at the start of the period.

Enter the following formula in a blank cell: =NPER(10%/12, -10000, 500000,,1). The value returned is *64.24* months. Here are some things to note regarding this example:

- The payment for the loan is a negative value (-10000), as this represents an outgoing payment.

- The payments are made monthly, so the annual interest rate of 10 percent is converted into a monthly rate (10%/12).

- The type argument is set to 1, as the payment is to be made at the beginning of each month.

- The value returned from the NPER function is in months, which is 64.24 months, which is the same as 5.35 years.

NPV Function

The NPV function is used to calculate the net present value of an investment based on a discount rate and a series of future payments (negative values) and incomes (positive values). Here, the cash flows are assumed to be periodic.

Syntax

=NPV(*rate, value1,* [*value2*], [*value3*], ... [*value254*])

The NPV function takes the following arguments:

- The first argument is the discount rate.

- Value1 to value254 is the list of numeric values representing payments and incomes.

- Negative values are treated as payments.

- Positive values are treated as income.

Example

Figure 11-5 shows examples of the NPV function.

◢	A	B	C
1			
2	Discount Rate	10%	10%
3	Initial investment	-$ 100,000.00	-$ 100,000.00
4	Return from 1st year	$ 32,500.00	$ 32,500.00
5	Return from 2nd year	$ 36,750.00	$ 36,750.00
6	Return from 3rd year	$ 42,600.00	$ 42,600.00
7	Return from 4th year	$ 46,800.00	$ 46,800.00
8	Return from 5th year	$ 50,400.00	$ 50,400.00
9		$ 50,166.21	$ 55,182.83

Figure 11-5. *NPV function*

In Figure 11-5, first let us look at the formula in cell B9, which is =NPV(B2,B3:B8). In this formula, the discount rate comes from cell B2 and the value arguments come from cells B3 to B8. This function gives the result *$50,166.21*. In this example, the initial investment of $100,000 (shown in cell B3), is made at the end of the first period. Therefore, this value is included as the first value argument to the NPV function.

In Figure 11-5, the formula in cell C9 is =NPV(C2,C4:C8)+C3. In this formula, the discount rate comes from cell C2 and the value arguments come from cells C4 to C8. This function gives the result *$55,182.83*. In this example, the initial investment of $100,000 (shown in cell C3) is made at the start of the first period. Therefore, this value is not included as the first value argument to the NPV function. Instead it is added to the NPV formula.

IRR Function

The IRR function returns the internal rate of return for a series of periodic cash flows. The internal rate of return (IRR) is widely used in business to choose between investments, as it indicates the profitability of an investment.

Syntax

=IRR(*values*, [*guess*])

The IRR function takes the following arguments:

- The first argument is an array of values or a reference to cells that contain numbers for which you want to calculate the internal rate of return. The values list must contain at least one positive value and one negative value to calculate the internal rate of return.

- The second argument is the initial guess of the expected IRR. This argument is optional. Starting with a guessed value given by the user, the IRR function cycles through the calculation until the result is within 0.00001 percent accuracy. If this argument is omitted, Excel will take it to be 10 percent. If the IRR function cannot find a working result after twenty tries, the *#NUM!* error value is returned.

Example

Figure 11-6 shows examples of the IRR function.

	A	B
1	Value	Comment
2	$ -100,000	Initial Investment
3	$ 18,000	1st year income
4	$ 26,000	2nd year income
5	$ 33,000	3rd year income
6	$ 28,000	4th year income
7	$ 43,000	5th year income
8		
9	-11%	IRR after 3 years
10	13%	IRR after 5 years

Figure 11-6. *IRR function*

In Figure 11-6, cell A2 shows the initial investment. Since this is a cash outflow, the value is negative. Cells A3 to A7 contain the expected income from the first year to the fifth year. In cell A9, we have used the formula =IRR(A2:A5). Here, we are trying to find out the internal rate of return for the initial investment of $-100,000 after three years. The value returned is *-11* percent. In cell A10, we have used the formula =IRR(A2:A7). Here, we are trying to find out the internal rate of return for the initial investment of $-100,000 after five years. The value returned is *13* percent. So, you can see that the IRR is negative after three years but is positive after five years. Since we have not used the guess argument, Excel takes 10 percent as the starting point for the iteration of up to twenty attempts to achieve the required accuracy. Being more accurate will make Excel faster and reduce the risk of getting a #NUM! error, but in most circumstances will not change the outcome of the result.

XIRR Function

The XIRR function returns the internal rate of return for a series of cash flows that are not periodic.

Syntax

=XIRR(*values, dates, [guess]*)

The XIRR function takes the following arguments:

- The first argument is an array of values or a reference to cells that contain numbers for which you want to calculate the internal rate of return. The values list must contain at least one positive value and one negative value to calculate the internal rate of return.

- The second argument is the series of dates corresponding to the values supplied.

- The third argument is the initial guess of the expected IRR. This argument is optional. Starting with the guessed value given by the user, the IRR function cycles through the calculation until the result is within 0.00001 percent accuracy. If this argument is omitted, Excel will take it to be 10 percent. If the IRR function cannot find a working result after twenty tries, the *#NUM!* error value is returned.

Example

Figure 11-7 shows an example of the XIRR function.

⊿	A	B	C
1	Value	Dates	Comment
2	$ -100,000	01-Feb-20	Initial Investment
3	$ 12,000	01-Apr-20	1st year income
4	$ 18,000	01-Aug-20	2nd year income
5	$ 23,000	01-Nov-20	3rd year income
6	$ 30,000	01-Jan-21	4th year income
7	$ 41,000	01-May-21	5th year income
8			
9	29%		XIRR after 5 years

Figure 11-7. *XIRR function*

In Figure 11-7, in cell A9 we have used the formula =XIRR(A2:A7,B2:B7).
This will return a value of *29* percent.

XNPV Function

The XNPV function is used to calculate the net present value of an
investment where the cash flows are not periodic.

Syntax

=XNPV(*rate, values, dates*)

The XNPV function takes three arguments, as follows:

- The first argument is the discount rate to be applied to
  the cash flows.

- The second argument is a series of cash flows. Negative
  values are treated as outflows and positive values are
  treated as inflows.

- The third argument is the series of dates for the cash flows. The length of the date series should be the same as the values series.

Example

Figure 11-8 shows an example of the XNPV function.

▲	A	B	C
1			
2	Discount Rate	10%	
3	Initial investment	-$ 100,000.00	01-Feb-20
4	Return from 1st year	$ 32,500.00	01-Apr-20
5	Return from 2nd year	$ 36,750.00	01-Aug-20
6	Return from 3rd year	$ 42,600.00	01-Nov-20
7	Return from 4th year	$ 46,800.00	01-Jan-21
8	Return from 5th year	$ 50,400.00	01-May-21
9		$ 94,331.65	

Figure 11-8. *XNPV function*

In Figure 11-8 in cell B8 we have used the formula =XNPV(B2,B3:B8,C3:C8). This will return the value *$94,332.65*.

Summary

In this chapter, we had a look at some of the financial functions available in Excel. As always, I suggest you try out the examples from this chapter using your own data and also using the different options for the arguments. This will give you more clarity regarding how the functions actually work.

In the next chapter, we will look into handling errors that occur in Excel formulas.

CHAPTER 12

Error Handling

In this chapter, we will look at different ways in which we can handle errors when they come up while using Excel functions.

Why Do Errors Occur While Using Excel Functions?

Errors occur in the following situations:

- Whenever arguments to Excel functions are not in the expected format; for example, if a function expects a number and the value supplied is not numeric. Therefore, Excel cannot evaluate the function, and this results in an error.

- An operation in Excel is invalid; for example, trying to divide a number by zero.

Different Types of Error Codes

Table 12-1 shows different kinds of error codes in Excel.

© Mandeep Mehta 2021
M. Mehta, *Microsoft Excel Functions Quick Reference*,
https://doi.org/10.1007/978-1-4842-6613-7_12

Table 12-1. *Error Codes in Excel*

Error Code	Description
#DIV/0	This error occurs when you tried to divide a number by zero.
#N/A	This error occurs when a value is not found.
#NAME?	This error occurs when you tried to use a non-existent named range or a function that does not exist.
#NUM!	This error occurs when numeric values used are invalid.
#REF!	This error occurs when a cell reference is removed.
#VALUE!	This error occurs when the data type of the function argument is different than expected. For example, a text string is supplied as an argument instead of a numeric value.
#NULL!	This error occurs when Excel is unable to figure out the range specified.
#SPILL!	This error occurs when a formula results in a spill range that runs into a cell that already contains data. In dynamic Excel, formulas that return multiple values will "spill" these values directly onto the worksheet. The range that encloses these values is called the spill range.
#CALC!	This error occurs when a formula encounters a calculation error with an array.

Note   #SPILL! and #CALC! errors are related to Excel 365 users with Dynamic Arrays enabled.

Functions Used to Handle Errors

There are a couple of functions used for error handling.

IFERROR Function

This is used to return a value when a formula results in an error. The IFERROR function has been widely used for error handling since it was introduced.

Syntax

```
=IFERROR(value, value to use in case of an error)
```

The IFERROR function expects two arguments, as follows:

- The first argument is a function/formula/reference that is checked for errors.
- The second argument is the value to be used in case the first argument evaluates to an error.

Example

Figure 12-1 shows an example of the IFERROR function.

Figure 12-1. *IFERROR function*

The function used in cell B2 is =IFERROR(10/0,"Error"). The value returned is *Error*. Here, we are trying to divide 10 by 0. This is an invalid operation. So, we get the error code *#DIV/0*. Since we have enclosed this equation inside the IFERROR function, the second argument of the IFERROR function is activated and the value *Error* is returned.

The function used in cell B3 is =IFERROR(10/5,"Error"). The value returned is 2. Here, we are trying to divide 10 by 5. This is a valid operation. Since the operation is valid, the second argument of the IFERROR function is not activated, and the value of the operation, *2*, is returned.

Table 12-2 shows other error-handling functions available that are not as frequently used.

Table 12-2. *Other Error-Handling Functions*

Function Name	Syntax
ISNA	=ISNA(*value*).
	Here, value can be cell/value/formula or a name range referring to cell/value/formula.
	Returns TRUE if the value is #N/A, else it returns FALSE.
ISERROR	=ISERROR(value)
	Here, value can be cell/value/formula or a name range referring to cell/value/formula.
	Returns TRUE if the value is an error, else it returns FALSE.

Debugging Excel Formulas
Using the F9 Key

Figure 12-2 shows an example of using the F9 key.

FIND	▼	:	×	✓	*fx*	=$B$1*$A2

◢	A	B	C	D	E
1	Table of 5	5			
2	1	$A2			
3	2	10			
4	3	15			
5	4	20			
6	5	25			
7	6	30			
8	7	35			
9	8	40			
10	9	45			
11	10	50			

Figure 12-2. *F9 key*

Select the formula as marked in the red box and press the F9 key to evaluate the formula. Ensure you press the Esc key or press the Ctrl+Z keys to remove the changes after using the F9 key, or else the changes will be made permanent and you will lose out on your formula.

Formula Tab

Figure 12-3 shows the options you can use to debug Excel formulas (marked in the red box)

Figure 12-3. *Debug Excel formula*

Let us look at some of the options available in the red box marked in Figure 12-3:

- **Trace Precedents** – This option displays arrows to cells that affect the current selected cell.

- **Trace Dependents** – This option displays arrows to cells that are dependent on the current selected cell.

- **Remove Arrows** – This option removes arrows displayed by the previous two options.

- **Show Formulas** – This option shows formulas in all cells containing formulas instead of the formula result.

- **Evaluate Formula** – This option allows you to evaluate a formula contained in a cell.

- **Error Checking** – The Error Checking dropdown has three options, as follows:

  - The first option is Error Checking - This option allows you to check for errors in the active sheet. When this option is selected, it displays the Error Checking dialog box if your worksheet contains errors. The first cell containing an error is selected when this dialog box is displayed. You can use this dialog box to find and investigate any errors one by one. Figure 12-4 shows the Error Checking dialog box.

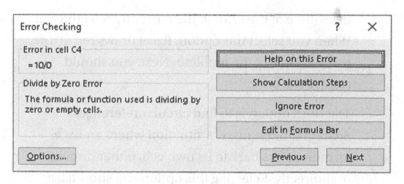

Figure 12-4. Error Checking dialog box

In this window, in the top-left corner, the actual contents of the cell are displayed, and below it is a short description of the error. In this case, it is division by zero. The buttons on this window are as follows:

- **Help on this Error** – This will display a help topic related to the specific type of error.

- **Show Calculation Steps** – This will display the Evaluate Formula dialog box.

- **Ignore Error** – Clicking this button will remove the green indicator from the top left-hand corner of the cell containing the current error.

- **Edit in Formula Bar** – This allows you to edit the formula in the formula bar. Click Resume to continue after you have made the changes.

- **Options** – This will display the Excel options.

- The **Previous** and **Next** buttons can be used to move between the errors on the active worksheet.

- The second option is Trace Error. For this option to work, ensure that your active cell is the cell containing an error. This option allows you to trace the source of the error in the currently selected cell. When you select this option, Excel draws red arrows to the source of the problem. Next, you should resolve the error.

- The third option is to find circular references. A circular reference is a situation where an Excel formula refers back to its own cell, either directly or indirectly. Selecting this option will show a list of cells with circular references. Clicking on the cell listed under Circular References will bring you exactly to that cell. Next up, you should resolve the circular references. You should try to avoid circular references in your sheets whenever possible.

Summary

To summarize, in this chapter we looked into how to handle errors while using Excel functions.

In the next chapter, we will look into the interesting concept of megaformulas.

CHAPTER 13

Megaformulas

In this chapter, we will look at a useful technique that combines several functions into a single formula. We can call it a megaformula. In other words, we have one or more functions nested inside other functions. The use of megaformulas is a contentious issue. Some people claim that having multiple intermediate formulas results in a clearer understanding of what is happening as compared to having a single complex formula. As a user, it's your call as to whether megaformulas would be helpful in your scenario.

What Is a Megaformula?

Many times, we use intermediate formulas in a worksheet to produce a result that we want. In other words, we have formulas that depend on other formulas. Once all these formulas are working correctly, we can remove all of these intermediate formulas and combine them to create a single large, complex formula. We can call such a formula a megaformula.

Advantages of Megaformulas

1. They use fewer cells, resulting in faster recalculations. This of course will depend on the specific scenario and the formulas used.

2. You can impress your boss and colleagues with your ability to build complex formulas.

© Mandeep Mehta 2021
M. Mehta, *Microsoft Excel Functions Quick Reference*,
https://doi.org/10.1007/978-1-4842-6613-7_13

Disadvantages of Megaformulas

1. The formula probably will be difficult to understand or modify, even for the creator of the megaformula.

Examples of Megaformulas

Now, let us look at some examples.

Dynamic Lookup Using INDEX MATCH Functions

Figure 13-1 shows an example of performing a lookup using INDEX and MATCH functions, where both the row number and the column number are gotten by using the MATCH functions.

	A	B	C	D
1	Roll No	Name	English	Maths
2	1	Roy	25	20
3	2	Dilip	15	18
4	3	Shalu	28	27
5	4	Mary	19	21
6				
7	Name	Shalu		
8	English	28		

Figure 13-1. *INDEX function with MATCH function*

In cell B8, we have used the formula =INDEX($A$1:$D$5,MATCH(B7,$B$1:$B$5,0),MATCH(A8,$A$1:$D$1,0)). Let us understand this formula:

1. The first argument to the INDEX function is the search range from A1 to D5. Note that we have used absolute reference for the search range.

2. The second argument to the INDEX function is
    MATCH(B7,$B$1:$B$5,0), Here, we are telling the
    MATCH function to find the value in cell B7 (*Shalu*)
    in the range B1 to B5. This will return *4*, as the value
    Shalu occurs in the fourth row of the search range
    B1 to B5.

3. The third argument to the INDEX function is
    MATCH(A8,$A$1:$D$1,0). Here, we are telling
    the MATCH function to find the value in cell A8
    (*English*) in the range A1 to D1. This will return *3*, as
    the value *English* occurs in the third column of the
    search range A1 to D1.

4. Now that we have the row and column references,
    we tell the INDEX function to return the cell value at
    the intersection of the fourth row and third column.
    This is the value in cell C4.

As you saw in this example we have the two MATCH functions nested
inside the INDEX function.

Create a Name Using the First Letter of the First Name and the Last Name

In this example, we will create a name using the first letter of the first name
and the last name. Figure 13-2 shows an example of this.

	A	B
1	Anupam Joshi	A Joshi
2	Mary Gomes	M Gomes
3	Rohit Sharma	R Sharma
4	Sunanda Patkar	S Patkar

Figure 13-2. Name example

In cells A1 to A4 we have names consisting of first name and last name. In cell B1 we have used the formula =LEFT(A1,1) & MID(A1, FIND(" ", A1), LEN(A1)). Copy the formula in cell B1 to cells B2 to B4.

Let us understand the formula as follows:

1. First, the function LEFT(A1,1) is evaluated. This will return the first character from cell A1, which is the first letter from the first name. This will return the value *A*.

2. Next, the formula FIND(" ", A1) is evaluated. This will find the position of the first space in cell A1. This will return 7.

3. The value returned in step 2 is used in the MID function as follows: MID(A1, 7, LEN(A1)). Here, we are saying return the text starting from position 7 till the end of the string (the end of the string is given by the function LEN(A1)). This will return the value *Joshi*.

4. The value returned in step 3 is joined using the ampersand (&) to the value returned in step 1.

The formula is evaluated as follows:

```
LEFT(A1,1) & MID(A1, FIND(" ", A1), LEN(A1))
↓
"A" & MID(A1, 7, LEN(A1))
↓
"A" & MID(A1, 7, 12)
↓
"A" & "Joshi"
↓
"A Joshi"
```

Create a Name Consisting of Only First and Last Name

In this example, we will create a name consisting of only the first and last names (Figure 13-3).

◢	A	B	C	D	E	F
1	Name	1st space	2nd space	first name	last name	First and last name
2	Anupam A Joshi	7	9	Anupam	Joshi	Anupam Joshi
3	Mary T Gomes	5	7	Mary	Gomes	Mary Gomes
4	Rohit R Sharma	6	8	Rohit	Sharma	Rohit Sharma
5	Sunanda S Patkar	8	10	Sunanda	Patkar	Sunanda Patkar

Figure 13-3. *How Excel will look with intermediate formulas*

Table 13-1 shows the formula used in cells B2 to F2.

Table 13-1. *Formula Used for Cells in Figure 13-3*

Cell Reference	Formula	Explanation
B2	=FIND(" ", A2)	Find the position of the first space in cell A1.
C2	=FIND(" ", A2, B2+1)	Find the position of the second space in cell A1.
D2	=LEFT(A2,B2-1)	Return the first name.
E2	=MID(A2,C2+1,LEN(A2))	Return the last name.
F2	=D2 & " " &E2	Combine the first name and last name separated by a space.

Copy the formulas in cells B2 to F2 to cells B3 to F5.

Now let us create a megaformula to eliminate the intermediate formulas. Enter the following formula in cell H2:

=MID(A2,1,FIND(" ", A2)-1) & " " & MID(A2,FIND(" ", A2, FIND(" ", A2)+1)+1,LEN(A2)). Copy this formula to the other cells.

As you can see, in this formula we have removed references to the cells containing the intermediate formulas (i.e., the cells B2 and C2). Figure 13-4 shows how the Excel screen will look with the megaformulas.

| H2 | ▾ | : | × | ✓ | fx | =MID(A2,1,FIND(" ", A2)-1) & " " & MID(A2,FIND(" ", A2, FIND(" ", A2)+1)+1,LEN(A2)) |

	A	B	C	D	E	F	G	H	I	J
1	Name	1st space	2nd space	first name	last name	First and last name		Mega formula		
2	Anupam A Joshi	7	9	Anupam	Joshi	Anupam Joshi		Anupam Joshi		
3	Mary T Gomes	5	7	Mary	Gomes	Mary Gomes		Mary Gomes		
4	Rohit R Sharma	6	8	Rohit	Sharma	Rohit Sharma		Rohit Sharma		
5	Sunanda S Patkar	8	10	Sunanda	Patkar	Sunanda Patkar		Sunanda Patkar		

Figure 13-4. *First and last names using a megaformula*

Reverse a Text String

In this example, we will see how to reverse a text string. Figure 13-5 shows how the example will look.

	A	B
1	Sachin Tendulkar	rakludneT nihcaS
2	Brian Lara	araL nairB
3	Rohit Sharma	amrahS tihoR
4	Ricky Ponting	gnitnoP ykciR
5	Andrew Flintoff	ffotnilF werdnA

Figure 13-5. *Reverse a string*

In cell B1, we have used the formula =TEXTJOIN("", 1, MID(A1, ABS(ROW(INDIRECT("1:" & LEN(A1))) - (LEN(A1) + 1)), 1)). For those of you who do not have Microsoft 365, after entering the formula, press Ctrl+Shift+Enter, as this is an array formula. For those of you who have Microsoft 365, you need to just press the Enter key, even for an array formula. Copy the formula in B1 to cells B2 to B5.

Let us understand this formula, as follows:

1. First, the formula will find the length of the string.

2. Based on the length of the string, the individual positions will be determined in reverse order.
   The part of the formula that does this is ABS(ROW (INDIRECT("1:" & LEN(A1))) - (LEN(A1) + 1)).

3. Next, each character is extracted using the MID function, starting from the last character to the first character.

4. Finally, each character extracted in step 3 is concatenated using the TEXTJOIN function.

The formula in cell B1 is evaluated as follows:

```
=TEXTJOIN("", 1,MID(A1, ABS(ROW(INDIRECT("1:" & LEN(A1))) -
                                (LEN(A1) + 1)), 1))
↓
=TEXTJOIN("", 1, MID(A1, ABS(ROW(INDIRECT("1:16"))) - (LEN(A1) + 1)) ,1))
↓
=TEXTJOIN("", 1, MID(A1, ABS({1;2;3;4;5;6;7;8;9;10;11;12;
                                13;14;15;16} - (16 + 1)), 1))
↓
=TEXTJOIN("", 1, MID(A1, ABS({1;2;3;4;5;6;7;8;9;10;11;12;
                                13;14;15;16} - (17)), 1))
↓
```

```
=TEXTJOIN("", 1, MID(A1, ABS({-16;-15;-14;-13;-12;-11;-10;-9;
                       -8;-7;-6;-5;-4;-3;-2;-1}), 1))
```
↓
```
=TEXTJOIN("", 1, MID(A1,{16;15;14;13;12;11;10;
                     9;8;7;6;5;4;3;2;1}, 1))
```
↓
```
=TEXTJOIN("", 1, {"r";"a";"k";"l";"u";"d";"n";"e";"T";"
             ";"n";"i";"h";"c";"a";"S"})
```
↓
```
rakludneT nihcaS, the final output of the formula.
```

Summary

In this chapter, we looked at megaformulas. As always, I suggest you try out the examples from this chapter using your own data and also using the different options for the arguments. This will give you more clarity regarding how the functions actually work.

In the next chapter, we will look into the interesting topic of array formulas.

CHAPTER 14

Array Formulas

In this chapter, we will take a look at array formulas.

Array formulas are an immensely powerful tool, but at the same time they are one of the most difficult concepts in Excel to master. A single Excel array formula can replace thousands of regular Excel formulas. However, most Excel users have never used array functions in their worksheets, as they are one of the most confusing Excel features to learn.

What Is an Array Formula?

An array consists of a group of data of the same type that is treated as one. An array formula considers the entire array as a single input to the formula. We use Ctrl+Shift+Enter to complete the array formula instead of just the Enter key. Since we use these keys to complete the formula, they are also known as CSE formulas.

Note Users with Excel 365 (the latest version of Excel) now have a feature called dynamic arrays. Basically, the dynamic array feature works as follows: whenever a formula is written, Excel determines if the formula can return multiple values. If there is the possibility that it could return multiple values, it will be saved as a dynamic array formula, which will be seen in older Excel versions as a legacy

---

© Mandeep Mehta 2021
M. Mehta, *Microsoft Excel Functions Quick Reference*,
https://doi.org/10.1007/978-1-4842-6613-7_14

CSE formula. Excel 365 users need to just press the Enter key instead of the Ctrl+Shift+Enter keys to complete the array formula. In this chapter, we will refer to versions other than Excel 365 as the traditional versions of Excel.

Advantages of Array Formulas

Some of the advantages of array formulas are as follows:

- Array formulas use less memory and are more efficient.

- It is not possible to change a single cell on its own within an array formula.

- Array formulas allow you to eliminate intermediate formulas.

- Array formulas allow you to perform some calculations that would be impossible using normal formulas.

Disadvantages of Array Formulas

Array formulas do have their downsides, like the following:

- Using a lot of large array formulas in a single workbook will increase the time for recalculations, thereby reducing workbook performance.

- Array formulas tend to make your formulas difficult to understand.

- You cannot use entire column references like "A:A" or "B:B" in your array formulas.

- You must always remember to press the Ctrl+Shift+Enter keys for array formulas or else you will get unexpected results. Excel 365 users do not need to press these keys for array formulas. They need to just press the Enter key.

Examples of Array Formulas

Let us now look at some examples of array formulas.

Count the Number of Characters in a Cell Range

Traditional Excel Version (Array Formula)

In this example, we will count the number of characters contained in all cells in a range. Figure 14-1 shows an example of this.

⧫	A
1	This is text
2	This is another line of text
3	This is the third line of text
4	
5	70

Figure 14-1. *Count the number of characters in a cell range*

As you can see, we have some text in cells A1 to A3. In cell A5, we have used the formula =SUM(LEN(A1:A3)). Remember to press the Ctrl+Shift+Enter keys to complete the formula instead of just the Enter key. The formula will appear in the formula bar as follows:

{=SUM(LEN(A1:A3))}

The curly braces ({}) are added automatically by Excel when you press the Ctrl+Shift+Enter keys.

Let us understand this formula. First, the inner LEN formula is evaluated. So, the LEN function returns the values *12*, *28*, and *30*, the lengths of the cells A1 to A3. All these values are passed on to the outer SUM function, which sums them up and returns the value *70* in cell A4. The formula is evaluated as follows:

```
{=SUM(LEN(A1:A3))}
↓
 =SUM({12, 28, 30})
↓
70→ the final return value.
```

Excel 365 Version (Array Formula)

For array formulas, Excel 365 users need to press only the Enter key instead of Ctrl+Shift+Enter. Figure 14-2 shows how the preceding example will work in Excel 365.

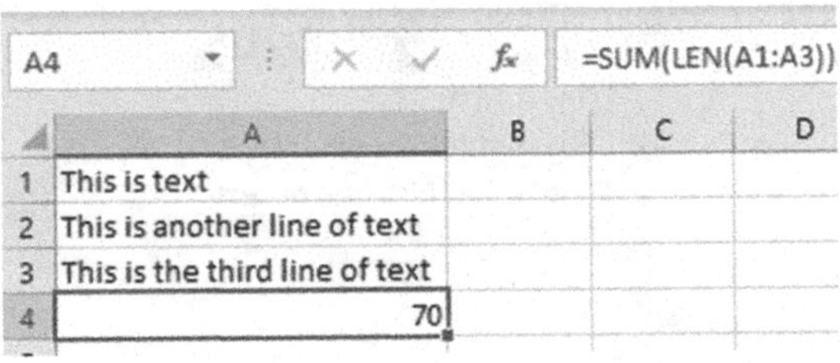

Figure 14-2. *Count the number of characters in a cell range (in Excel 365)*

In cell A4, we have used the formula =SUM(LEN(A1:A3)). After entering the formula, Excel 365 users will just press the Enter key. As you can see, Excel 365 does not add the curly braces ({}) like in the previous example.

Without Array Formula

Now let us look at the approach to get the count of the number of characters in a cell range without using an array formula. This will work in both traditional Excel as well as Excel 365.

Figure 14-3 shows how Excel will look without the array formula.

	A	B
1	This is text	12
2	This is another line of text	28
3	This is the third line of text	30
4		70

Figure 14-3. *Without array formula*

In cell B1, we have used the function =LEN(A1). Copy the formula in cell B1 to cells B2 and B3. We have used the LEN function in cells B1 to B3 to get the length of the text in cells A1 to A3. In cell B4 we have used the function =SUM(B1:B3). This will return the sum of the lengths of the text strings stored in cells B1 to B3. This without-array-formula approach will work in traditional Excel as well as in Excel 365.

So, we have seen two approaches to counting the number of characters in a cell range, the first using an array formula and the second using regular formulas. The difference between the two approaches is that in the array-formula approach, you can eliminate the step to get the length of individual cells. But at the same time, the second approach is easy to understand and maintain.

Find the Three Largest Numbers
Traditional Excel Version

Now, let us see another example of an array formula in which we find the highest three grades earned in math class. Figure 14-4 shows how Excel will look to get the three largest numbers using an array formula.

We have the data in cells A1 to A10. Next, select cells C1 to C3 and write the following formula in the formula bar: =LARGE(A1:A10,{1;2;3}). Remember to press Ctrl+Shift+Enter to complete the formula instead of just the Enter key. The formula will appear in the formula bar as follows:

{ =LARGE(A1:A10,{1;2;3}) }

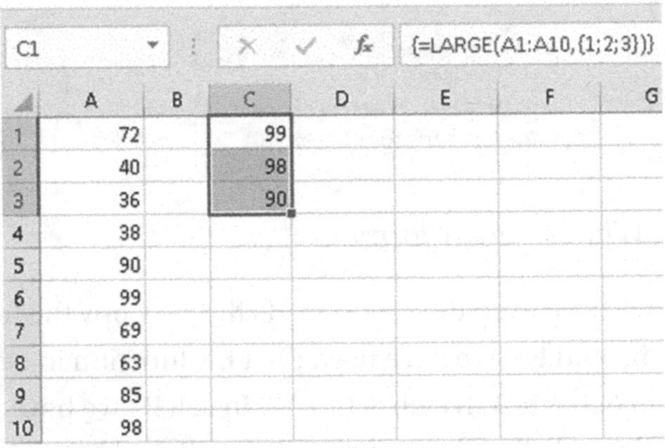

Figure 14-4. *Three largest numbers using an array formula*

Let us understand this formula. Notice we have used {1;2;3} as the second argument for the LARGE function. This is an array constant. Array constants are always enclosed inside curly braces ({}). As we want multiple values to be returned, we have enclosed the positions we want returned in curly braces, separated by a semi-colon (;).

Separating the values using a semi-colon will return the values in rows. Separating the values using a comma will return the values in columns.

Note   While using array constants as arguments, ensure that the appropriate number of cells in either rows or columns are preselected before executing the array formula, or else you could get unexpected results. In the preceding example, we selected cells C1 to C3 before executing the formula.

Now, select cells D1 to F1 and write the following formula in the formula bar: =LARGE(A1:A10,{1,2,3}). Remember to press Ctrl+Shift+Enter to complete the formula instead of just the Enter key. The formula will appear in the formula bar as follows:

{ =LARGE(A1:A10,{1,2,3}) }

This will return the values column-wise, as can be seen in Figure 14-5.

D1			×	✓	f_x	{=LARGE(A1:A10,{1,2,3})}	
◢	A	B	C	D	E	F	G
1	72		99	99	98	90	
2	40		98				
3	36		90				
4	38						
5	90						
6	99						
7	69						
8	63						
9	85						
10	98						

Figure 14-5. *Three largest numbers, column-wise*

Excel 365 Version

Figure 14-6 shows how the examples will work in Excel 365.

B1	▼	⋮	×	✓	*fx*	=LARGE(A1:A10,{1;2;3})	

◢	A	B	C	D	E	F
1	72	99				
2	40	98				
3	36	90				
4	38					
5	90					
6	99					
7	69					
8	63					
9	85					
10	98					

Figure 14-6. *Three largest numbers in Excel 365*

In Figure 14-6, in cell B1, we have used the formula =LARGE(A1:A10, {1;2;3}). After entering the formula, Excel 365 users will just press the Enter key. As you can see in Figure 14-6, Excel 365 does not add the curly braces ({}) like in the previous example for the traditional version.

Now, select cell D1 and write the following formula in the formula bar: =LARGE(A1:A10,{1,2,3}). Remember to press the Enter key. The formula will appear in the formula bar as follows, without the curly braces:

=LARGE(A1:A10,{1,2,3})

This will return the values column-wise, as can be seen in Figure 14-7.

D1	▼	:	×	✓	*fx*	=LARGE(A1:A10,{1,2,3})	

◢	A	B	C	D	E	F
1	72	99		99	98	90
2	40	98				
3	36	90				
4	38					
5	90					
6	99					
7	69					
8	63					
9	85					
10	98					

Figure 14-7. *Three largest numbers, column-wise*

Sum the Three Largest Numbers

Traditional Excel Version

Now let us extend the previous example. Instead of just *getting* the top three marks, we will *sum* the top three marks. Figure 14-8 shows an example for summing the three largest numbers.

D1	▼	:	×	✓	*fx*	{=SUM(LARGE(A1:A10,{1;2;3}))}	

◢	A	B	C	D	E	F	G
1	72		99	287			
2	40		98				
3	36		90				
4	38						
5	90						
6	99						
7	69						
8	63						
9	85						
10	98						

Figure 14-8. *Sum the three largest numbers*

As you can see in Figure 14-8, in cell D1 we have used the formula =SUM(LARGE(A1:A10,{1;2;3})). Remember to press Ctrl+Shift+Enter to complete the formula instead of just the Enter key.

The formula will appear in the formula bar as follows:

```
{ =SUM(LARGE(A1:A10,{1;2;3}) )}
The formula will be evaluated as follows
{ =SUM(LARGE(A1:A10,{1;2;3}) )}
↓
{ =SUM(99,98,90)}
↓
287
```

Excel 365 Version

Figure 14-9 shows how the previous example will look in Excel 365.

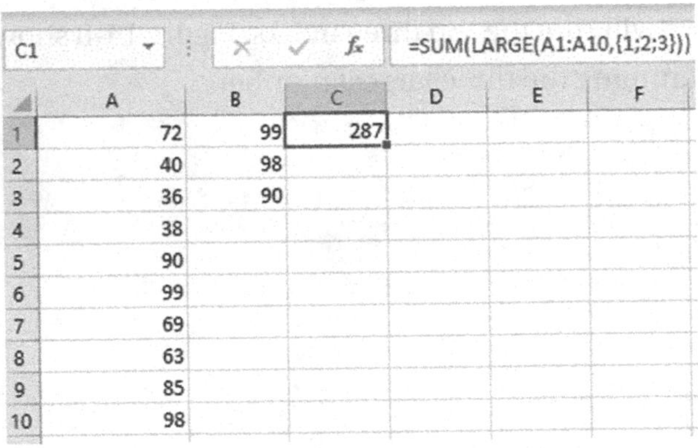

Figure 14-9. Sum the three largest numbers

In Figure 14-9, in cell C1, we enter the formula =SUM(LARGE(A1:A10, {1;2;3})) and press the Enter key. The formula will appear in the formula bar as follows, without the curly braces:

=SUM(LARGE(A1:A10,{1;2;3}))

This will return the value *287*, as can be seen in Figure 14-9.

Find Unique Values

In this example, we will use an array formula to find unique values from a list.

Traditional Excel Version

Figure 14-10 shows how Excel should look for this example.

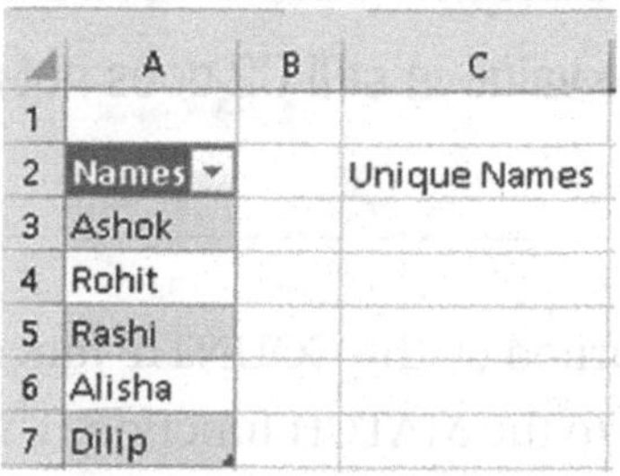

***Figure 14-10.** Excel screen for unique names after entering data*

Cell A2 contains the heading. We have our data in cells A3 to A7. In cell C2, we enter the text "Unique Names." We have named the cell range from A2 to A7 *mydata*. In cell C3, enter the formula =IFERROR(INDEX (mydata[Names], MATCH(0,COUNTIF($C$2:C2, mydata[Names]), 0)), ""). Remember to press Ctrl+Shift+Enter to complete the formula instead of just the Enter key.

The formula will appear in the formula bar as follows:

`{ =IFERROR(INDEX(mydata[Names], MATCH(0,COUNTIF($C$2:C2, mydata[Names]), 0)), "")}`

Let us examine this formula.

1. `COUNTIF($C$2:C2,mydata[Names]),0)` – Counts the number of times the items in the unique list appear in the main list, which is the *Names* column of the *mydata* table. It will return the array *{0;0;0;0;0;0}*. We are using an expanding reference for the range `$C$2:C2`. In an expanding reference, the starting cell is absolute while the ending cell is relative. So, as the formula is copied down, the reference will expand to include more rows in the unique list.

Note   Ensure that the value in cell C2 does not appear in the main list.

---

2. The value returned by the COUNTIF function in step 1 is passed on to the MATCH function. The MATCH function will locate the items by looking for a count of zero. It always returns the first match when there are duplicates. The MATCH function for cell C3 will be evaluated as `MATCH(0,{0;0;0;0;0;0},0))`. For cell C3, the MATCH function will return the value *1*.

3. Finally, the value returned by the MATCH function in step 2 is passed on to the INDEX function as a row number, and the INDEX function will return the name at that position. The INDEX function for cell C3 is evaluated as `INDEX(mydata[Names],1)`.

4. We are enclosing the INDEX function inside the IFERROR function to handle any error, in which case an empty string is returned.

Now, copy the formula in cell C3 to cells C4 to C10.

Note   Ensure that there are no blank cells in the table *mydata*.

Figure 14-11 shows the Excel screen after implementing the array formula for unique values.

| C3 | ▼ | : | × | ✓ | *fx* | {=IFERROR(INDEX(mydata[Names],MATCH(0,COUNTIF($C$2:C2, mydata[Names]),0)),"")} |

▲	A	B	C	D	E	F	G
1							
2	Names ▼		Unique Names				
3	Ashok		Ashok				
4	Rohit		Rohit				
5	Rashi		Rashi				
6	Alisha		Alisha				
7	Dilip		Dilip				
8	Ashok						

Figure 14-11. *Unique values after array formula is evaluated*

Excel 365 Version

Excel 365 users can use the UNIQUE function to get unique values from a given list. The UNIQUE function is available only in Excel 365. Figure 14-12 shows an example of the UNIQUE function.

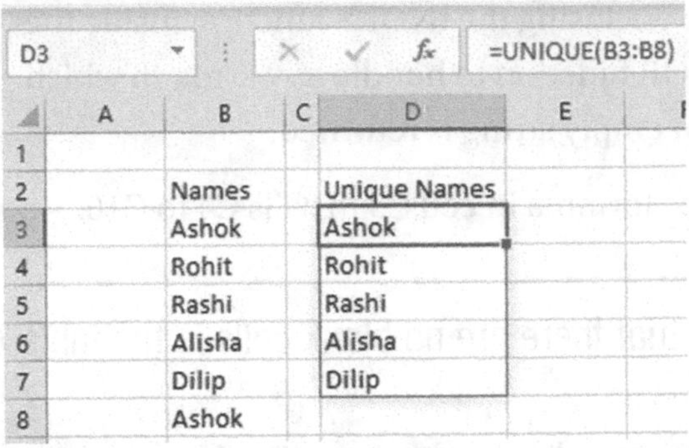

Figure 14-12. *UNIQUE function*

In cells B3 to B8 we have a list of names. In cell D3, we have used the function =UNIQUE(B3:B8). The UNIQUE function returns a list of unique values.

Multiplication Table in Excel Created Using Array Formulas

Traditional Excel Version

In this example, we will create a multiplication table using array formula. Figure 14-13 shows an example of a multiplication table in Excel using an array formula.

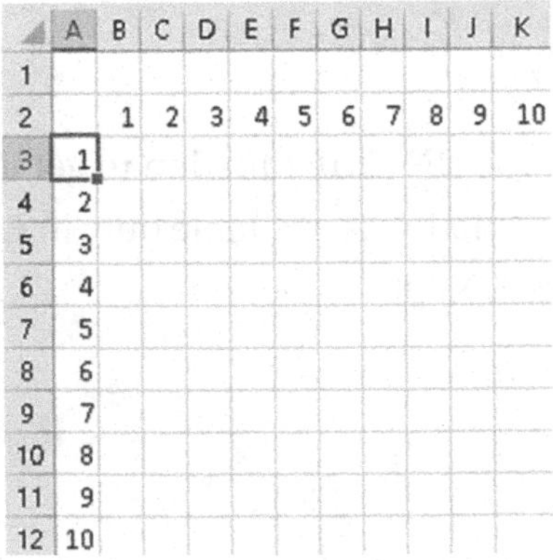

Figure 14-13. *Multiplication table created using array formula*

In Figure 14-13, we have the values from 1 to 10 in the cells B2 to K2 and A3 to A12. Now, select cells B3 to K12, as seen in Figure 14-14.

Figure 14-14. *Selected cells for multiplication tables created using array formula*

Keeping the cells selected, enter the following formula in the formula bar: =A3:A12*B2:K2. Remember to press Ctrl+Shift+Enter to complete the formula instead of just the Enter key. The formula will appear in the formula bar as follows:

{=A3:A12*B2:K2}

Figure 14-15 shows the completed multiplication table created using an array formula.

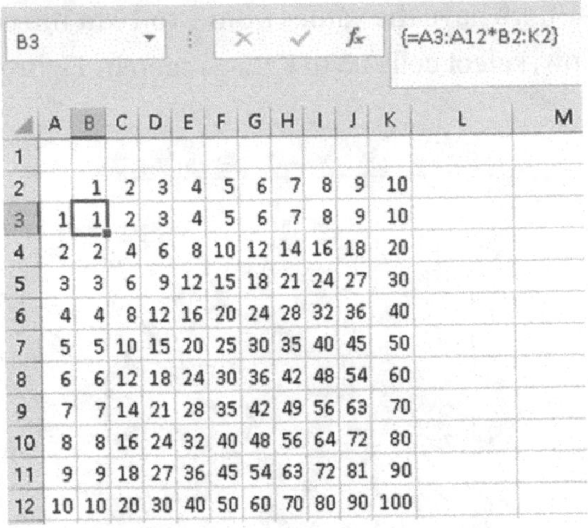

B3 {=A3:A12*B2:K2}

	A	B	C	D	E	F	G	H	I	J	K	L	M
1													
2		1	2	3	4	5	6	7	8	9	10		
3	1	1	2	3	4	5	6	7	8	9	10		
4	2	2	4	6	8	10	12	14	16	18	20		
5	3	3	6	9	12	15	18	21	24	27	30		
6	4	4	8	12	16	20	24	28	32	36	40		
7	5	5	10	15	20	25	30	35	40	45	50		
8	6	6	12	18	24	30	36	42	48	54	60		
9	7	7	14	21	28	35	42	49	56	63	70		
10	8	8	16	24	32	40	48	56	64	72	80		
11	9	9	18	27	36	45	54	63	72	81	90		
12	10	10	20	30	40	50	60	70	80	90	100		

Figure 14-15. *Completed multiplication table created using array formula*

Excel 365 Version

Figure 14-16 shows an example of the multiplication table in Excel created using an array formula.

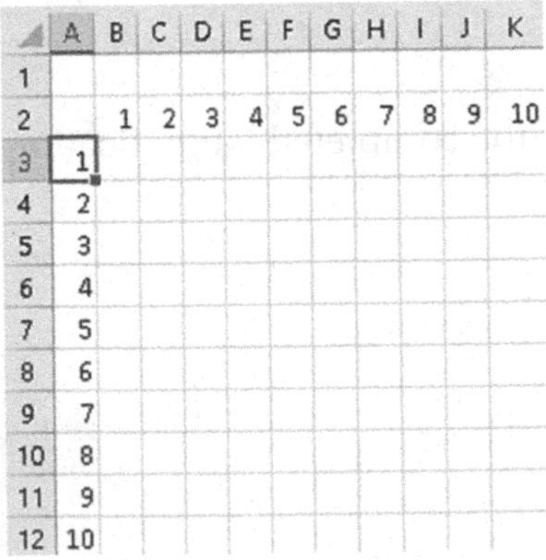

	A	B	C	D	E	F	G	H	I	J	K
1											
2		1	2	3	4	5	6	7	8	9	10
3	1										
4	2										
5	3										
6	4										
7	5										
8	6										
9	7										
10	8										
11	9										
12	10										

Figure 14-16. *Multiplication table using array formula*

In Figure 14-16, we have the values from 1 to 10 in the cells B2 to K2 and A3 to A12. Now, select the cells B3 to K12, as seen in Figure 14-17.

Figure 14-17. *Selected cells for multiplication table using array formulas*

Keeping the cells selected, enter the following formula in the formula bar: =A3:A12*B2:K2. Remember to press the Enter key to complete the formula. The formula will appear in the formula bar as follows:

=A3:A12*B2:K2

Figure 14-18 shows the completed multiplication table created using an array formula.

B2#		fx	=A2:A11*B1:K1							
	A	B	C	D	E	F	G	H	I	J	K
1		1	2	3	4	5	6	7	8	9	10
2	1	1	2	3	4	5	6	7	8	9	10
3	2	2	4	6	8	10	12	14	16	18	20
4	3	3	6	9	12	15	18	21	24	27	30
5	4	4	8	12	16	20	24	28	32	36	40
6	5	5	10	15	20	25	30	35	40	45	50
7	6	6	12	18	24	30	36	42	48	54	60
8	7	7	14	21	28	35	42	49	56	63	70
9	8	8	16	24	32	40	48	56	64	72	80
10	9	9	18	27	36	45	54	63	72	81	90
11	10	10	20	30	40	50	60	70	80	90	100

Figure 14-18. *Multiplication table in Excel 365*

So, in the preceding examples we saw some of the ways in which array formulas can be used in Excel. With newer releases of Excel, Microsoft has not only updated the calculation engine but also provided a lot of new functions that can replace array formulas, thereby making the array formulas easier to understand and maintain.

EXCEL 365 Functions

Let us look at some more of the array functions available only in Excel 365. The following functions are not available in traditional Excel.

SORT Function

The SORT function sorts a list of names in ascending or descending order.

Syntax

```
=SORT(array, [sort index], [sort order], [by col]).
```

The SORT function takes the following arguments:

- The first argument is an array of values or a range of cells to sort. These values can be text, numbers, dates, times, etc.

- The second argument is the sort index. This argument is optional. The value will be an integer that tells by which column or row to sort. If this argument is omitted, the default index of 1 is used.

- The third argument is the sort order. This argument is optional. It can take one of the following two values:

- 1 - The values will be sorted in ascending order. This is the default value if the third argument is omitted.

- -1 - The values will be sorted in descending order.

- The fourth argument specifies whether the sorting is to be done by rows or by columns. This argument is optional. It can take the following values:

- FALSE - The values are sorted by row. This is the default value if the fourth argument is omitted.

- TRUE - The values are sorted by column.

Figure 14-19 shows an example of the SORT function.

B3	▼	⋮	✕	✓	*fx*	=SORT(A3:A7)

◢	A	B	C	D
1				
2	Unsorted Names	Sorted Names		
3	Ashok	Alisha		
4	Rohit	Ashok		
5	Rashi	Dilip		
6	Alisha	Rashi		
7	Dilip	Rohit		

Figure 14-19. *SORT function*

In Figure 14-19, cells A3 to A7 contain an unsorted list of names. In cell B3, we have used the formula =SORT(A3:A7). This will return a sorted list of names in cells B3 to B7.

SORTBY Function

The SORTBY function is used to sort a range of cells based on the values in another range or array.

Syntax

=SORTBY(*cell range* , *sort array1*, [*sort order1*], [*sort array2*, sort order2*],...)

The SORTBY function takes the following arguments:

- The first argument is the cell range or the array of values to sort.

- The second argument is the cell range or array to sort by.

- The third argument is the sort order. This argument is optional. It can take one of the following two values:

  - 1 - The values will be sorted in ascending order. This is the default value if the third argument is omitted.

  - -1 - The values will be sorted in descending order.

- Sort array2 / Sort order2, ... - These are the additional array/cell range and sort pairs that are used for sorting. These arguments are optional.

Figure 14-20 shows an example of the SORTBY function.

D3	▼	:	×	✓	fx	=SORTBY(A3:B7,B3:B7)

◢	A	B	C	D	E	F	G	H
1								
2	Names	Marks		Names	Marks			
3	Ashok	79		Dilip	71			
4	Rohit	95		Rashi	77			
5	Rashi	77		Ashok	79			
6	Alisha	80		Alisha	80			
7	Dilip	71		Rohit	95			

Figure 14-20. *SORTBY function*

In Figure 14-20, in cells A3 to A7, we have the names of students, and cells B3 to B7 contain the grades. In cell D2 we have used the formula =SORTBY(A3:B7,B3:B7). This will return the names sorted by grades in ascending order, as can be seen in Figure 14-20 in the cells D3 to E7.

SEQUENCE Function

The SEQUENCE function is used to generate a sequence of numbers.

Syntax

=SEQUENCE(rows, [columns], [start], [step])

The SEQUENCE function takes the following arguments:

- The first argument specifies the number of rows to be filled.

- The second argument specifies the number of columns to be filled. This argument is optional. If this argument is omitted, it defaults to 1 column.

- The third argument specifies the starting value for the sequence. This argument is optional. If this argument is omitted, the sequence will start from 1.

241

- The fourth argument specifies the increment for each subsequent value in the sequence. This argument is optional. If this argument is omitted, the step value will be 1. If a positive value is used for this argument, the subsequent values will increase, thereby creating an ascending sequence. If a negative value is used, the subsequent values will decrease, thereby creating a descending sequence.

Figure 14-21 shows an example of the SEQUENCE function.

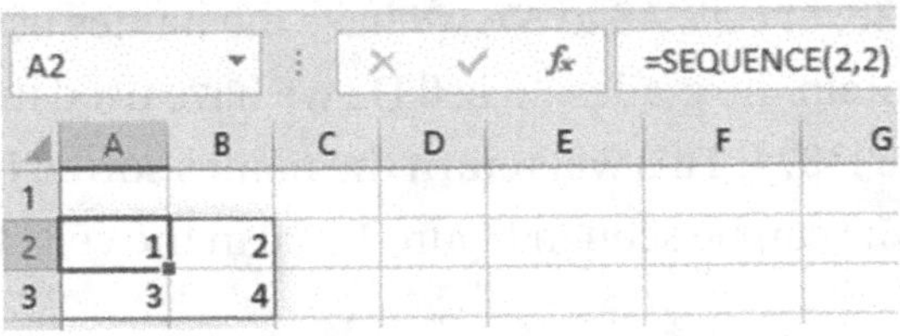

Figure 14-21. *SEQUENCE function*

In cell A2, we have used the formula =SEQUENCE(2,2). This will create a sequence of four numbers consisting of two rows and two columns, as can be seen in Figure 14-21.

Summary

In this chapter, we touched on the topic of array formulas in Excel. As always, I suggest you try out the examples from this chapter using your own data and also using the different options for the arguments. This will give you more clarity regarding how the functions work.

With this, we come to the end of our journey through Excel formulas. I hope you have enjoyed it as much as I enjoyed it bringing it to you.

Formula Ready Reckoner

This appendix contains a list of all the functions covered in this book. The functions are arranged alphabetically and grouped by the category of the Excel function.

Table A-1. *Text Functions*

Function Name	Use
CONCATENATE or &	Join two or more strings.
EXACT	Check if two strings are an exact match.
FIND	Return the position of one string inside another. The search is case sensitive.
LEFT	Return characters from the left of a string.
LEN	Return the length of a string.
LOWER	Convert text to lowercase.
MID	Return characters from middle of a string.
PROPER	Convert text to proper case, where the first character of each word is in uppercase.

(continued)

© Mandeep Mehta 2021
M. Mehta, *Microsoft Excel Functions Quick Reference*,
https://doi.org/10.1007/978-1-4842-6613-7

Table A-1. (*continued*)

Function Name	Use
REPLACE	Replace part of a string with another string.
REPT	Repeat one or more characters.
RIGHT	Return characters from the right of a string.
SEARCH	Return the position of one string inside another. The search is not case sensitive.
SUBSTITUTE	Replace part of a string with another string.
T	Check if the argument passed to it is a text.
TEXT	Convert a number or a date to a text in a specified format.
TEXTJOIN	Join text from multiple strings. The text is separated by a specified delimiter.
TRIM	Remove extra spaces from a string.
UPPER	Convert text to uppercase.
VALUE	Convert a number in text format to an actual number.

Table A-2. *Date Functions*

Function Name	Use
DATE	Create a date.
DATEDIF	Calculate the difference between two dates in terms of complete days, months, and years.
DATEVALUE	Create a date from a text string.
DAY	Return the day part from a specified date.
EDATE	Return a date that is given months from a specified date.
EOMONTH	Return the last day of the month that is given months before/after a specified date.
MONTH	Return the month part from a specified date.
NETWORKDAYS	Return the number of workdays between two dates while at the same time ignoring specified holidays.
TODAY	Return the current system date.
WEEKDAY	Return the weekday of a specified date.
WEEKNUM	Return the week number of a specified date.
WORKDAY	Calculate a date that is a specified number of workdays in the past or the future based on a specified date.
YEAR	Return the year part from a specified date.

Table A-3. *Time Functions*

Function Name	Use
HOUR	Return the hour part of a date time.
MINUTE	Return the minute part of a date time.
NOW	Return the current system date and time.
SECOND	Return the second part of a date time.
TIME	Create the time.
TIMEVALUE	Create the time from a text string.

Table A-4. *Lookups and Reference Functions*

Function Name	Use
ADDRESS	Return the cell reference in text format.
CHOOSE	Return a value from a list of values based on a specified position.
COLUMN	Return the column number.
COLUMNS	Return the number of columns in a specified range.
FORMULATEXT	Return the formula of a specified cell in text format.
HLOOKUP	Look up a value in horizontal ranges.
INDEX	Return the value at the intersection of a specified row and column.
INDIRECT	Convert a text string into a cell reference.
MATCH	Look up the relative position of the value in a specified row or column.
OFFSET	Return a cell range containing one or more cells starting from a specified cell reference.
ROW	Return the row number.
ROWS	Return the number of rows in a specified range.
VLOOKUP	Look up a value in vertical ranges.

Table A-5. *Aggregate Functions*

Function Name	Use
AGGREGATE	Perform various aggregation methods of a range of cells.
AVERAGE	Perform average of numeric values in a cell range.
AVERAGEIF	Perform average of numeric values in a cell range based on a condition.
AVERAGEIFS	Perform average of numeric values in a cell range based on one or more conditions.
COUNT	Count the number of numeric values in a cell range.
COUNTA	Count the number of cells in a cell range that are not empty.
COUNTBLANK	Count the number of cells in a cell range that are empty.
COUNTIF	Count the number of numeric values in a cell range based on a condition.
COUNTIFS	Count the number of numeric values in a cell range based on one or more conditions.
MAX	Return the maximum number from a set of numbers.
MAXIFS	Find the maximum value from a range based on one or more conditions.
MIN	Return the minimum number from a set of numbers.
MINIFS	Find the minimum value from a range based on one or more conditions.
SUBTOTAL	Perform various aggregation methods of a range of cells.
SUM	Sum a range of cells.
SUMIF	Sum a range of cells based on a condition.
SUMIFS	Sum a range of cells based on one or more conditions.
SUMPRODUCT	Return the sum of the products of arrays.

Table A-6. *Logical Functions*

Function Name	Use
AND	Return TRUE if all conditions are TRUE, else return a FALSE.
IF	Evaluate a condition and perform an action if the condition is true or perform some other action if the condition is false.
IFS	Evaluate multiple conditions and return a value that corresponds to the first TRUE condition.
NOT	Convert the TRUE value to FALSE and the FALSE value to TRUE.
OR	Return TRUE if any of the conditions are TRUE, else return FALSE.
SWITCH	Compare one value against a list of values, and return a result corresponding to the first matching value.
XOR	Return TRUE if any of the conditions are TRUE. Return FALSE if all conditions are TRUE.

Table A-7. *Maths Functions*

Function Name	Use
ABS	Return the absolute number.
CEILING	Round up a number to the nearest specified multiple.
FLOOR	Round down a number to the nearest specified multiple.
INT	Return the integer part of a decimal number rounded to the nearest integer.
RAND	Generate a random number that is >= 0 and <1.
RANDBETWEEN	Generate a random whole number between two specified numbers.
ROUND	Round a number to a specific number of digits.
TRUNC	Truncate a decimal number to a specified number of digits.

Table A-8. *Information Functions*

Function Name	Use
CELL	Return information about a cell.
INFO	Return information about the current operating environment.
ISBLANK	Check if a cell is blank or not.
ISERROR	Check if a value is an error or not.
ISEVEN	Check if a value is an even number or not.
ISFORMULA	Check if the cell reference is a formula.
ISLOGICAL	Check if the specified value is either TRUE or FALSE.
ISNA	Return TRUE if the value passed contains #N/A, else return FALSE.
ISNONTEXT	Check if the value contains a text or not.
ISNUMBER	Check if the value contains a number or not.
ISODD	Checks if a value is an odd number or not.
ISREF	Check if the value passed is a reference.
ISTEXT	Check if the value contains a text or not.
N	Convert the value passed to a number.
NA	Generate the #N/A error to indicate value not available.
SHEET	Return the sheet number of the referenced sheet.
SHEETS	Return the number of sheets in the reference.
TYPE	Return a numeric code depending on the type of a value in a cell.

Table A-9. *Financial Functions*

Function Name	Use
FV	Return the future value of an investment that has periodic constant payments and a constant interest rate.
IPMT	Return the interest payment based on a series of future payments.
IRR	Return the Internal Rate of Return for a series of periodic cash flows.
NPER	Calculate the number of periods required to pay off a loan wherein the periodic payment amount and interest rate are constant.
NPV	Calculate the net present value of an investment.
PMT	Calculate the periodic payment value based on a series of future payments.
PPMT	Return the principal payment based on a series of future payments.
PV	Return the present value of an investment based on a series of future payments.
RATE	Calculate the interest rate that would be required to pay off a loan.
XIRR	Return the Internal Rate of Return for a series of cash flows that are not periodic.
XNPV	Calculate the net present value of an investment where the cash flows are not periodic.

Table A-10. *Error Functions*

Function Name	Use
IFERROR	Return a custom value when an error occurs in the specified formula.
ISNA	Return TRUE if the value passed contains #N/A, else return FALSE.
ISERROR	Return TRUE if the value passed contains an error, else it returns FALSE.

Index

© Mandeep Mehta 2021
M. Mehta, *Microsoft Excel Functions Quick Reference*,
https://doi.org/10.1007/978-1-4842-6613-7

Printed in the United States
By Bookmasters